Gene Krcelic

LOVES LIKE A HURRICANE

When God Whispers in the Dark

AMBASSADOR INTERNATIONAL
GREENVILLE, SOUTH CAROLINA & BELFAST, NORTHERN IRELAND

www.ambassador-international.com

Loves Like a Hurricane
When God Whispers In The Dark

ISBN: 9781935507604

Cover Design & Page Layout by David Siglin

AMBASSADOR INTERNATIONAL
Emerald House
427 Wade Hampton Blvd.
Greenville, SC 29609, USA
www.ambassador-international.com

AMBASSADOR BOOKS
The Mount
2 Woodstock Link
Belfast, BT6 8DD, Northern Ireland, UK
www.ambassador-international.com

The colophon is a trademark of Ambassador

DEDICATION

For Mary.
And for Caroline and Alexis,
and their children, and their children's children . . .

Endorsements for Gene Krcelic

"I tend to trust individuals who have been there, done that versus those who simply preach. Gene Krcelic is a man I would follow into battle any day of the week. Loves Like a Hurricane is a real, transparent sharing of one man's understanding of God and His love for each of us."

—MIKE NOVAK

PRESIDENT / CEO, K-LOVE / AIR 1

"The cool of a Beat poet, the soul of a Monk, and the scholarly trappings of a Professor, Gene Krcelic speaks with clarity and force, while bouncing his wisdom in a rhythm that keeps you awake. Langston Hughes meets Thomas Merton is the best way I can describe my friend. Turn up the volume on this book, you're about to hear reverent joy in stereo."

—JOEY ELWOOD

PRESIDENT, GOTEE RECORDS

"What I love about Gene is that he will always do the heavy lifting. He takes on the tough assignments, the challenging problems, the big issues, and the hard choices. The difference between Gene and other heavy lifters is that he is typically doing the hard stuff to impact other people. Gene is passionate to live life with integrity and purpose. He is willing to find the needle or move the mountain, so that others will benefit. He is vigorous in serving others and his ferociousness in doing good. Gene is a gamer who looks to lift others up. Lead on my brother..."

—STEVE BIONDO

PRESIDENT, THE JAMES FUND

Table of Contents

Further Endorsements

"Gene is a man who appears to always be looking for a way to be of help. Whether it is in the aftermath of a natural disaster or a friend in need, he seeks to find a way to come alongside. This propensity to 'search' reveals his kind heart that has been sought out and found by a God who looks for the lost sheep and the lost coin. It is a privilege to know a man who lives a life of service in gratitude for his own rescue."

—Al Andrews
Director, Porter's Call

"With rare honesty and blunt-spoken candor Gene Krcelic tells how God's sovereign purposes have been taking shape amid the whirlwind of his own life. In so doing he invites and encourages the reader to attend to the wondrous and unexpected ways by which the living God is at work in the tempest of our own lives forming and reforming each of us to serve as instruments of God's will in the world."

—Rev. Dr. Allen C. McSween

Foreword

I'VE HEARD PEOPLE LAUGH AT God. The idea of Him seems ridiculous and somehow humorous to some. Unseen, unheard, yet supposed to be obeyed? The arrogance of man leaves us to think that we can do this thing called life just fine on our own. When life is good, business is successful, and family is healthy, why in the world would we lay everything down for a cross? It's laughable, right?

Sometimes we meet someone who immediately causes us to think, "This is someone I need to know. This is a person with a story worth hearing." This was my "blink" impression of Gene Krcelic.

During the summer of 2010, I was working at Camp Electric in Nashville, TN. The summer camp, hosted by tobyMac, gives young aspiring musicians the opportunity to learn directly from their favorite artists. (Think "School of Rock" for Christian teenagers.) I met some incredible people that week, but the one who most piqued my curiosity was definitely Gene. Our meeting seemed chance and was very brief (we spent about fifteen minutes sitting around a table in a board room with a few other people, counting money we'd just raised to build a school in Nicaragua). All I knew after that first encounter was that Gene was the president of the Premier Foundation, dressed like James Bond, and was someone I needed to know more about. I eagerly pocketed his business card.

As fate or, as I prefer, providence would have it, I spent the rest of that year working in Gene's hometown of Greenville, SC. I wasted no time in calling him and setting up a meeting. Our coffee mugs were steaming as we delved into general small talk and basic get-to-know-you questions and answers. He is a family man with a wife and two daughters. He loves people. He travels constantly. He's passionate about music, a piece of information which was reinforced by his inability to stop humming twangy country tunes from the Darius Rucker show he had attended the previous evening.

By the time we rounded our second course of lattes, my curiosity was burning. This man had a story, my intuition assured me, and I needed to hear it. So I asked. We quickly graduated from the surface and fell into the depths of Gene's life. Without any pretense, embarrassment, or apologies, he shared his story with me. Flattering or not, he was consistently open and honest. He was real. I was encouraged. I was inspired. To put it simply, I was moved. He wasn't afraid to reveal his past because he was secure in his present and future. Starbucks witnessed a connection of souls that day, and three and a half hours later, lattes stone cold, we walked away bonded for life.

That first meeting with Gene set the tone for our friendship. When he shared with me his plan for this book, I was not only eager to read it myself but excited to have an easy means of sharing his story with others, knowing it would prove as relevant to them as it is to me. I was thrilled to find that when I finally held the finished manuscript, his story resounded with me just as honest and sincere on the page as it did in person across a table in a coffee shop. It was Gene in black and white.

Loves Like a Hurricane is, in short, a story about the journey we all make called life. It's an authentic and brutally honest look into the footprints of our lives. It's a beautiful narrative of how the connections we make and relationships we cultivate affect us, whether we are aware of it or not. It is full of candid stories that may make you laugh, cry, or perhaps want to throw something. Gene will challenge you to think a little differently about the world in which we live, about the lives we affect and those that affect us.

Loves Like a Hurricane is an honest and refreshing perspective on life, Christianity, and religion in general. The French aviator and author de Saint-Exupery once said that "A designer knows he has achieved perfection not when there is nothing left to add, but when there is nothing left to take away." Gene practices Christianity in its most elementary form: love. Love God, love others. What could be simpler?

Gene has stripped away all the religious mumbo jumbo and found that life *without* God is the joke. Nothing brings clarity like staring death in the face. It's suddenly laughably obvious that we are in desperate need of a Savior.

—**KENWORTH REEVES, JR.**
Global Non-Profit Strategist

Introduction

My intent was to write a book I could give to my children and say, "Here, this is a large part of my faith journey. This will give you some insight into who your dad was and who he is today and why I am who I am when it comes to believing in God and Jesus Christ. I hope it helps." Then perhaps they would pass it to their children and so on.

I am not so bold as to think my life is any more interesting than that of the person standing next to me at the grocery store checkout line. I think every person's life is a worthwhile best-seller; it's just up to each person to tell his own story. I do feel that there were times in my life and faith journey, as told, that a reader may see and be able to identify with. Perhaps it will offer someone encouragement in times of distress or hope for a stronger faith in God. It's simply how I dealt with things and how things dealt with me.

I have taken the time to connect the dots of my life, and it has been a gift to me. My reflection led me down memory lane, taking turns down side streets I had forgotten about. As I took the stroll, I realized there were a lot more people who helped shape my faith than I had remembered. In fact, it became clear that every person I have met, every song I have listened to, every book I have read, and everyone and everything that has touched my life has helped shape my beliefs and values in some way. Knowing this, it became abundantly clear that the same is true in reverse—with everything I touch and everyone I encounter, I will have a hand in shaping beliefs and values. The same truth holds true for all of us.

Music has played an enormous part in my life. Being the youngest of four children, I was not only blessed with my parent's love for jazz and the great vocal standards, I had the albums of older brothers and sisters to learn from. God knew what He was doing when He gave me zero musical talent. My ego would have been out of control. I can't sing very well nor can I play any instrument; I just love music.

In the pages to follow, I quote a few musicians and songwriters because they have helped inspire me. Music is a powerful tool. Music is an important art form that allows us to express ourselves when we are personally at a loss for words. It has also helped shape who I am today. One artist I didn't quote in the chapters of this book is Trevor Hall. Although I don't know him personally and don't know for certain where he stands regarding faith, his music is beautiful. In my favorite song of his, "House," I see myself in the lyrics. It embodies my journey in so many ways. Here is a sample:

> *over the oceans and seas they were, they were searching for me*
> *but I hid in the crest of a wave, protected by the Lion's mane*
> *humbled by the sight and the sound*
> *let me tell you of the love I have found*
> *I heard of a House, where death cannot enter any more*
> *many rooms in this mansion all covered in gold*
> *Sits upon a land where misery has lost its grip*
> *and the rains they shower all our fear away*
> *well my body said just turn and run*
> *but then I felt the light of the sun*
> *in the heart that I thought had just died*

started coming slowly alive
we awoke in the mansion above
and called it love[1]

In addition to the thousands of musical artists and songs that have contributed to my life, there are a number of people I failed to mention or thank in this book. Quite frankly, there are too many deserving recognition to note. I have also changed the names of some people. The journey as told here is to the best of my recollection; others may remember some of the facts differently.

Preface

It is during our darkest moments that we must focus to see the light.
—ARISTOTLE ONASSIS[2]

I THOUGHT I WAS GOING to die on August 31, 2005.

I lay motionless in bed and had resigned myself to death when I felt an overwhelming sense of the end rush upon me with the paralyzing force of a boa constrictor. In what seemed like forty eternities as I prepared for death, I stopped the inevitable. I prayed and I fought. I focused and searched for the light. In those brief moments I found the Truth I was searching for over the span of my life. For the first time in my wandering existence, I knew where I would spend eternity. My storm had cleared.

Six hundred miles away leaving the Gulf of Mexico, Hurricane Katrina was also clearing. After wreaking devastating havoc on New Orleans and other Gulf communities, it had been downgraded from a hurricane to a tropical depression. On August 31, 2005, it dissipated and vanished into a Canadian sky with a slight whisper. The storm claimed nearly 2,000 lives and damaged or destroyed 150,000 homes as over 80 percent of New Orleans treaded water. Hurricane Katrina was the largest natural disaster in the recorded history of the United States. The storm had cleared.

I had no interest in New Orleans. No reason to care. The terror of the Superdome was merely a series of stories on the evening news. New Orleans was a world away. It was a bad situation, but not my situation.

Without even knowing, that stormy summer night, Katrina and I danced. In the years to come, Katrina would make me stare into the mirror and answer my own questions. The reality of my own death altered my perspective of God, while the reality of post-Katrina New Orleans altered my perspective of me.

August 31, 2005, changed my life forever.

Call me Hurricane.

The Night

Because I could not stop for Death,
He kindly stopped for me
—EMILY DICKINSON[3]

SOMETIMES GOD RAPS GENTLY AT the door, but we don't know it's Him, so we ignore the disturbance. He whispers through the door, but His words fall on deaf ears.

A few years later, He knocks again, a little louder.

"Go away—I'm busy," we can be heard saying as we tend to our usual routine.

The knocks keep coming, but the door is never opened. His voice grows louder, but we run from the message.

He beats on the door even harder and more frequently. His presence is known, but still we turn our heads and ignore Him standing in the portal to our room. "Not now—I have other things more important to tend to. Stop bothering me."

God doesn't leave. He is still there watching, caring, loving. He doesn't intrude because He knows it's not time. The whole while, He wants to make sure we know He is there but gives us time to recognize Him and realize that the knock is real and He is there . . . waiting. He knows timing is everything.

The knocks increase and are not only known—they are felt. But still, we turn away.

Then, there is silence.

Where did He go?

All is still.

Finally, as sure as the candle lights the dark, the door is kicked open and there is no running from His presence, His power, His grace. God enters the room at the moment He knows we are ready. He grabs our heart and fills it with His love for us, igniting the fire in our souls that can never be extinguished. We become one with God.

God knows when we are ready.

Timing is everything.

: : : : : :

So this is what it feels like when you're dying, I thought, staring into black. *This is it!*

Lying on my back, eyes wide open, I felt a light, cool breeze on the back of my head like that of an angel whistling in my direction, without the sound. The ever-present tension in my neck began to seep into my left shoulder. It trickled into my bicep, curling around my elbow like a garden serpent, and shot deep through my forearm. The numbing tingle reached its final destination, my fingertips. I was motionless.

My brain began to throb as pearls of cold sweat speckled my forehead. Cold and clammy, I felt a wave of nausea brush across my throat. I was paralyzed. I was wide awake. I thought that if I could only get to the bathroom and splash some cold water on my face I could revive, snap back into reality. But I couldn't move. Frozen, facing the prospect of death, I talked to God. It was time.

My mind, my heart raged for clarification. I demanded the truth of my future, the truth of the present. *How will it end?* I frantically thought. But my questions swept me to 35,000 feet, coach class. I remembered the moment I had first felt that wisp of cold air on the top of my head, crammed into the back of a U.S. Airlines return flight from New York—the same breeze. I thought it was an open air vent pointed toward my head. As I reached up to close it, I saw the vent was already shut, but the breeze sensation continued.

That's odd, I had thought. *Odd.*

In an instant, my thoughts rested on my heart. I could hear my heart crying out like a haunting tell-tale Edgar Allen Poe novel. With the clarity of panic, I saw the truth. *Perhaps the cool sensation on my head was the beginning of a stroke, or the onset of a heart attack, or a brain tumor, or the predecessor to an aneurism.* I remembered my high school classmate who was the model of health and fitness but tragically died of a brain aneurism shortly after our five-year class reunion. She and I had a lot in common in high school. There was a synergy between us; perhaps it was our senior-superlative "Most Egotistical." Was this the typical end for vanity?

My mind raced back to my bedroom and the still of the room. A clamor in my head, striding in unison with my wife's melodic breathing. Mary, my loving wife of soon-to-be eighteen years, was cradled in a deep rhythmic sleep. She inhaled a deep breath in and pushed a steady breath out . . . a deep breath in and a steady exhale out. Mary was not a deep sleeper, so the last thing I wanted to do was to wake her out of this rare REM slumber, even if I was dying.

This epic battle between life and death volleyed for what seemed like hours but was surely only minutes. The hurricane that had ravaged New Orleans just two days earlier entered my home with no regard for my family. Soaking wet from the cold sweats, I prepared for death and all that it meant. The other side, the next step, the better place, heaven, hell, nothing—I prepared to take the step without waking up Mary.

At first, I was entangled in the web of fear. The fear of leaving my life unresolved without having the opportunity to say goodbye. But the fear waned. It subsided and dissipated like Hurricane Katrina gusting across the hemlock treetops over Canada. My fear was gone. I was at peace with eternity. I was at peace with God. There was no question where I was going to spend the rest of eternity, in the warmth of God's soul. He let me know that everything was going to be okay, but He just didn't tell me if I was going to make it out of my bedroom alive.

As my soul yearned eternal, my heart continued to bang against my chest. Although my everlasting was confirmed, there were unresolved issues. I was sad. I thought of waking up Mary to call EMS but I did not want to cause a scene and freak her out. I knew she would be okay. My insurance coverage was recently raised to a comfortable amount so she and the girls would not need to worry about financial security.

The girls.

What will the girls do without their father?

A vivid scene played out in my mind, a vision, an apparition. I was looking down, live and in person, as if the Ghost of Christmas Future was holding my hand. The scene was set on my driveway. A cold steel stretcher was being rolled down the cracked cement driveway by two EMS workers. On top of the stretcher was a black zippered bag and inside the bag was the body of me. Standing by the house were Caroline and Alexis crying uncontrollably and Mary trying to keep it together for her girls. The play was real, it was sharp, and it was riveting. It scared me. Death no longer concerned me; I knew where I was headed. I would be fine. The thought of my ten-year-old and thirteen-year-old daughters standing there was horrifying. I knew Mary would be okay, but what about my girls?

With my heart rate at a sprinter's high and sweat saturating my pillow, I figured it was time to fight. I was prepared for heaven and looking forward to sitting in the lap of God; I wasn't prepared to leave my family behind.

It was time to call 9-1-1 to summon the ambulance and see if they could get me to the hospital quick enough to save me. It was time to wake up Mary.

With bold courage I fought to break the python-like stranglehold on my body. I was now prepared to wake up my wife. I didn't want to startle her. I knew she wasn't going to be happy with the situation, so I had to ease her into the fact that I was on the brink of death; but it was time to fight for life.

With God's hand guiding mine, I touched Mary on the arm.

"Mary, wake up! Mary!"

She wasn't too pleased as I woke her from a deep sleep. I felt bad because she hadn't been sleeping well recently and I knew that restful sleep was a precious commodity.

"What? What's wrong?" she mumbled.

It was like magic. As soon as I touched her arm, my pain eased. The cold sweat subsided and a restful peace engulfed me. It was as if I had touched Jesus' robe and I was healed.

"Ahhh, nothing," I said with surprise and a strange sense of relief.

"No, what's wrong?"

"No, I'm fine."

By this time she was wide awake and wondering why I had just jolted her out of a blissful dream. The cat was out of the bag! I had no choice but to admit to my frenzy.

"I'm okay now. I just thought I was dying," I said with cool reassurance as if nothing had happened.

"Are you serious?!"

"Yeah, but it's all good now. Go back to sleep."

After the full story, we went to sleep. A deep, restful, blissful REM sleep. At least I did.

Finally, after years of uncertainty and searching, I knew I had found my place with God. I knew that no matter what happened to me in my life I would be resting in heaven one day. Not just an imaginary hopeful place that we dream of when we convince ourselves that there is life after death—I was certain that I would be living with God.

No more life after death, but life after life.

Now with the security of everlasting knowledge, God had granted me some additional time on earth. My responsibility shifted from *what can I do for me* to *what can I do for others*. I asked myself, "Would I be able to recognize my footprint on this planet when I look down from heaven? Will the world be a better place because I have lived? How would my community look if I had never lived?" The questions echoed in my ears. My heart shifted. My mind shifted. My actions shifted.

I needed to make sure my footprint would be as recognizable as Neil Armstrong's on the surface of the moon. I was prepared to stomp the ground.

: : : : : :

God watched me patiently as He saw me meander through decades of ignorance and defiance. I scurried away from His whispers to blaze a path dictated by my own plan. He allowed me to stray but made sure the seed of hope stayed firmly planted in my heart.

He watched as I endured hard, valuable lessons that would, one day, pay off for His glory. The lessons would temper me as a sword gains its true strength only by being exposed to the flames of the furnace. He turned me from a non-believer who scoffed at His efforts to a vocal and loyal instrument of His love.

As a young boy and later a man, I grew to hate the word *Christian* from years of exposure to overzealous Christian ministers. I ran from them and their plan for mankind as I continued to write my own plan for my life. But I was empty, so I searched. Ever so slightly a new plan was revealing itself to me.

The final piece of the puzzle was put into place. It took a storm of biblical proportion for me to look into the eyes of young children and elderly hurricane survivors in Alabama to see my real future. God's plan for my life was finally revealed to me in a post-hurricane apocalypse while I was a servant to my fellow man through a Presbyterian church relief effort.

God lit the fire in my heart and I was finally burning for Him and His Son. I always thought that my years of agnostic denial made me an unlikely torchbearer for Jesus Christ; on the contrary, those years would become the fuel that would keep the torch burning to light the way so others would see.

The torch was lit the night I thought I was dying, but it took a string of improbable events to really set it ablaze.

The Wonder Years

If you're not a born-again Christian, you're a failure as a human being.
—Reverend Jerry Falwell[4]

THINGS STARTED TO GET STRANGE for me in fourth grade.

Dead babies. That's what they were advertising: dead babies.

It really didn't matter what it was, as long as it was dead. Dead frogs, dead cats, and dead squirrels were all intriguing . . . but dead babies! That's a grand slam. On a Sunday night, there was no way *The Wonderful World of Disney* and *Mutual of Omaha's Wild Kingdom* could compete with seeing something your parents would never approve of, no matter how liberal they were. Dead babies were big, even if it was just pictures.

Telling a ten-year-old boy he can see anything dead, as long as a friend comes along, was like discovering King Tut's tomb in his backyard. He wanted to tell everyone but knew if the word got out to too many people it wouldn't be secretive and forbidden anymore. Friends would start bringing friends, and then even worse, they might start bringing their sisters.

It was always a giveaway that something no good was going on when a pile of one-speed Schwinn banana seat bikes stacked up in Bill's front yard. The second sign was that the boys who belonged to those bikes were not seen or heard. That's because in the backyard someone was trying to burn a hole through a firecracker with a magnifying glass or strike a match to the Pall Mall I swiped from my mom's jeweled cigarette case. It was always fun watching Steve gag and cough from inhaling a big puff on the cigarette, while we hoped he might throw up.

Sometimes a daring volunteer would borrow a few magazines from his father's bottom drawer. We would congregate in the basement and make-believe we were married to Miss May, Miss June, or Miss July. Ah, the wonder years!

Every now and then we would conspire to take the new kid who just moved into the neighborhood on a midnight snipe hunt in the peach orchard. We would all sleep over in the big blue canvas tent in my backyard then head to the woods. There's nothing more fearless than a ten-year-old boy standing in the woods with a grocery sack, getting ready to catch a ferocious snipe, all alone under a peach tree.

When the last snipe hunter got back to the tent, the night was far from over. The first person asleep could count on waking up with his hand in a bowl of warm water and a soaking wet sleeping bag. You never wanted to be the first person to doze off at a sleepover in my neighborhood.

A pile of one-speed Schwinn banana seat bikes in Bill's front yard was never a good sign. That's why the invitation to see the dead babies was always a one-on-one covert operation.

"Don't tell anyone," they would whisper. "Especially don't tell your parents!"

That's why "the ask" to go to Timmy's house was so important as to not create undue parental suspicion.

"Mom," I'd say with a pleading yet confident tone, "A bunch of guys are going over to Timmy's house tonight, kind of like a youth group or something . . . can I go?"

"Will his parents be there?" my mom would sternly inquire, knowing that she saw a pile of bikes just yesterday.

"I definitely think they will be there."

"Okay. Be careful and be home by nine."

Perfect!

My mom always told me to be careful. Ever since the incident in Florida, she knew I had a nose for getting into things I shouldn't. On a warm Florida Sunday afternoon, Mike and I went exploring at the construction site between our houses. A new patio home was in the process of being built. There was a fresh, new, four-foot-high pallet of cinderblocks stacked neatly in a square. A pile of cement blocks and a five-year-old boy . . . that was a bad combination. I wanted to climb to the top and conquer the mound—wasn't that why the pile was there in the first place? As I reached for the top block, I grabbed it firmly, and it started to slide in my direction. I pulled it off, fell on my back, and the block smashed on my face.

As a parent myself, I can now appreciate the terror in my mother's eyes when her baby boy walked into the kitchen with his face and clothes covered in blood. My dad said I was the nicest and most calm little boy for a couple of weeks after the cinderblock incident. Maybe the block-on-the-face memory was why she told me to be careful.

On the way over to Timmy's dead baby viewing parlor, we would talk about what was on the schedule for the evening. For the first-timers like me, there was always the basic run down on what to expect.

"At the beginning, everyone will sit in a room and talk for a while, getting to know the other kids and youth leaders," I was told. "They're really nice."

Homemade chocolate chip cookies with real Coca-Cola would be a definite part of the evening's festivities. That was always a treat for most kids in our neighborhood because nearly all families would drink Check Cola, or on a special occasion R.C. Kool-Aid was the beverage of choice in our refrigerator. We never had real Coke at our house that I can remember.

We walked to the house through the yard where we played football most afternoons and every weekend, the same one where Scott ran right into the pine tree and started to cry right before he called me a Polack. That was yesterday.

I began to get a little nervous. The thought of seeing pictures of dead babies was neat a couple of hours ago, but now that it was actually getting closer, it made my stomach jump around, kind of like puffing on the Pall Mall.

"Then they will talk to us for a while before we see the pictures," he continued.

That seems reasonable enough, I thought.

The advisors were going to prepare us before they broke out the goods, the pictures of the dead babies. Make sure everyone knew where the bathrooms were in case the sissies couldn't handle it.

"Then after we see the pictures they will talk to us some more about some stuff then we'll go home."

It was normal operating procedure for a youth group I guess, seeing as I had never been to a youth group before.

The preparation was over and I found myself standing on the concrete slab in front of the aluminum screen door.

"We're here," he said.

I was where I knew I wasn't supposed to be. I wasn't drinking Boone's Farm Apple Wine in the woods like my brother or sneaking a smoke like my sister. I was only going to look at some pictures . . . of dead babies.

We pushed the orange dot next to the screen door and the bell chimed.

The door swung open.

"Hello, welcome!"

: : : : : :

I could see a bunch of people milling around inside talking and smiling a lot, but it was pretty calm. I was the new kid so I thought I was better off seen and not heard. The lady who answered the door had a strange Stepford gaze to her eyes, not like she had been doing drugs or anything; it was just a bit peculiar. She was holding a book in her hand. It had a soft cover and it bent and flopped around when she held it. On the book, gold lettering read *Holy Bible*. We had one of those in our house, but it was a lot bigger, a big, white, leather-covered Bible in the center of our parlor table. In the front of it was an outline for our family tree. Our Bible was holy. So holy that it made me a little nervous to even touch it, and of course we never opened it up and read from it. It was the sacred *Holy Bible*. I would never hold it and let it flop around in my hand like she did, even if it wasn't so huge or didn't have a hard cover.

Our hostess welcomed us inside, and we went directly to the basement where the kids were hanging out. There was an abundance of cookies and Coke for everyone, just as promised. We hung out sitting on the freshly raked red shag carpet as I was introduced to a bunch of people. It was odd because I knew most of the kids from the neighborhood and these weren't them.

Finally an older man, maybe twenty-two or twenty-eight years old, came into the room and started talking about all sorts of things, things that a kid with ADD had a hard time following. Back then, there was no universally accepted condition described as Attention Deficit Disorder; it was simply called Not Paying Attention and the prescription was simply a spanking with a leather belt. I didn't want to hear all of the other stuff as he waved his Bible in the air; I wanted to see the dead babies.

He pulled out a book and opened it to where a few pictures were inserted. He gently took the 8 x 10 pictures out of the book and passed them around one by one.

Pretty cool, I thought.

But the hands and feet of the babies were so small they couldn't have been real babies. I had seen a real baby before and the hands and feet were a lot bigger in real life. The youth advisor talked about how these babies were murdered by their mother by a thing called abortion. I had never heard of abortion before and really didn't know what he was talking about. My ADD was all over the place with the overload of this new information.

After the advisor gathered up the gruesome pictures, he talked to us about Jesus. He had us all bow our heads and say a prayer with him. He prayed about how we are all sinners and how murdering unborn babies was a sin. I wasn't sold on the fact that I was a sinner; I was just a ten-year-old boy who loved football and got into trouble from time to time, but I sure wasn't any baby killer.

He then asked if we wanted a personal relationship with Jesus Christ. And that if we wanted Christ in our hearts and to have Him as our personal Savior we should raise our hands and say a silent prayer after him. I peeked as everyone's head was bowed and saw a few hands lifted in the air. *So*, I thought. *Why not? I'm in.* I raised my hand and said the prayer. They called it the sinner's prayer. That was simple. I didn't feel any different. Should I have?

I came to find out I now had a new label . . . a born-again Christian.

Ordinarily, my new label would have been fine, but the word *Christian* is something you never said in my house. It was the ultimate four-letter word. We were Catholics, not Christians.

The Landing

There is only one religion, though there are a hundred versions of it.
—George Bernard Shaw[5]

In the 70's in Lynchburg, Virginia, you were either labeled a "born-again Christian" or not a Christian at all. There was no middle ground. It was a lot for a boy striding through puberty to try and figure out. I just wanted to play football. I had enough on my mind, like trying not to get caught after dark in the yard of the old Civil War–era house across the street. Rumor had it that there was a murder on the top floor after the war and the ghost of the young female victim could be seen walking around in the house during a full moon. I needed to keep most of my attention on the lunar cycle and not on Christianity.

We were Roman Catholic and members of Holy Cross Catholic Church where we attended our usual Sunday mass. As with most kids, it was a struggle to just get though the mass with all of the standing up and sitting down and kneeling. It was a rare occasion that Father Ron would deliver a sermon that captured and held my ADD in check. But every now and then he would connect and keep my attention. Father Ron was relatively young, nice looking, and quite charismatic; well, as charismatic as a Catholic priest could be.

The reward for getting through mass was a weekly trip to the bowling alley. Every Sunday, my parents would take us bowling for a few games. It was a sport in which I excelled. Golf wasn't a part of our recreation; it cost too much money and took too much time. Besides, golf was for the rich people. My parents were in bowling leagues, so I grew up a bowling alley rat joining any league my parents could afford. In fact, Jerry Falwell Jr. was even in the same bowling league as I was. It was always exciting getting to bowl against the son of the most famous person in Lynchburg.

When our teams met on the lane, Jerry Jr. and I never talked about religion, abortion, being born-again, democrats or republicans, the moral majority, or any of the other things our parents found to be eminently interesting and important. We just wanted to beat each other on the oiled hardwood.

Even though it never occurred to me to label someone because of their beliefs, their heritage, or skin color, it was only a matter of time before I would be singled out because my great-grandmother was born in Poland. Other kids thought it was funny to call me a Polack and tell Polack jokes around a group of other kids. Someone had to bear the brunt of adolescent shenanigans, and no black people lived in the neighborhood just yet. My mother would always suffer the greatest pain when she caught wind of it. She shed too many tears caused by the verbal arrows of others. She was proud of her grandmother's country and took keen offense to any verbal assault.

My closest neighborhood friend thought it would be funny to show me a trick he learned. I loved a good trick. He filled up a bowl with cold water and took a salt shaker and covered the top of the water with salt.

"Those are all the white people," he said, trying to keep in his laughter.

Then he grabbed the pepper shaker. "Those are all of the black people." But he wasn't so kind in their description.

"Then," he reached for the Palmolive. He squeezed a single drop of dishwashing liquid into the bowl. "That's the Polack!"

he said with loud, boisterous laughter. As the soap hit the salt and peppered water, all of the spice sped away from the dish-washing liquid like they were running from the plague. I really never understood why my best friend would show me this trick, knowing that I was the dish soap in his magic trick. I was proud of who my ancestors were and couldn't understand why my great-grandmother being from Poland was so degrading. The irony was that people thought my last name was Polish, when in fact it was Croatian. Who's the idiot now? Hatred and hurtful humor tended to be colored by ignorance.

Being the brunt of tasteless jokes flowed from house to house and from kid to kid. I received a reprieve on the Polack jokes when the first black family moved into the neighborhood. There was a buzz around the neighborhood that a black family was moving in and everyone said that was a bad thing. In my house my parents never shared the sentiment. In fact, if the "N" word was ever ut-tered, it was a sure strapping from my father. I was blessed with a race- and color-neutral family. My father grew up in a Jewish neighborhood, and one of his closest friends was a black man that married a white woman. That's why my parents were so distressed years earlier in Florida when they awoke to a burning cross in our neighbor's yard. A white family had helped a black man and the local Ku Klux Klan wizard wanted it known that that kind of behavior would not be tolerated in Titusville, Florida.

Tolerance of others was king in our house. With the exception of Republicans, members of Thomas Road Baptist Church, and the fledgling Liberty Baptist College. Richland Hills was directly across the street from the old Brookville Middle School, the first home of Falwell's new venture, Liberty.

As a residual benefit of living in Richland Hills, the neighbor-hood was a testing ground for Jerry's soldiers for Christ. On at least a weekly basis, our doorbell would ring and there would be a couple of young, well-dressed college students carrying a couple of those floppy Bibles. The negotiation to come inside the house was always colored by who answered the door. If they were lucky, my sister would answer and they would usually find themselves standing on the landing of our split-foyer home. On more than one occasion I passed by from the kitchen to the basement hearing my sister recant the sinner's prayer with eyes closed and hands to the sky. Tears would hit the rug normally occupied by our pet English Setter, Candy. Candy liked to guard the front door, until someone knocked.

The landing, as we called it, was a place of saving grace, terror, fear, and sadness. It was the portal from which my parents threw my brother, Louie, out of the house for causing so much pain and upheaval in our family. It wasn't necessarily from selling drugs out of the house, or totaling countless cars, or having bouts with the police. It was a culmination of it all! One of the final straws was when I opened the front door and looked across the yard to the edge of the road. My brother was lying on the ground in a lifeless pose. I thought for sure my brother was dead. Was he hit by a car, was it a drug overdose, or what was it? Later we found out his "friends" had dropped him off onto the road after he had passed out. Nonetheless, standing on the landing, I thought my brother was dead, and my parents had had enough.

My mother stood strong under all circumstances. She had to because my father traveled so much, striving to make a better life for our family. He went where his business took him. One evening, my sister's friend pulled into our gravel driveway. There were banging and screams coming from behind the front door. We all ran to see what was going on in the front yard. I opened the door and her friend was screaming as she ran into the house. There was a man behind her with a pistol in his hand. She screamed, "He's got a gun, he's got a gun!"

Mom's motherly instinct kicked in as she slammed our door and locked it before the man could get inside. Mom then shielded her body over the door in case he shot through it. She wanted to make sure the bullets didn't hit any of her children as she yelled at us to get in our rooms. The assailant was the boyfriend of my sister's friend. He had followed her to our house and was harassing her, so she pulled a gun on him from under her driver's seat. He snatched it from her and then chased her to our door. I always wondered why someone would pull a gun on someone else if they didn't intend to pull the trigger.

There were a lot of life's lessons and ponderings that took place on the linoleum landing. In fact, it was the very location of my second born-again experience. My parents were not in the house, so when the doorbell rang, I let the two Caucasian, white-shirted college students into the house. We stood on the landing, and they asked me so many questions.

""Do you know where you are going when you die?"

"Why do you think you are going to heaven?"

"Are you saved?"

"Do you know Christ as your personal Lord and Savior?"

"Would you like to have a personal relationship with Jesus Christ?"

My responses were your standard non-Christian responses.

"I'm going to heaven."

"Because I'm a good person."

"I think I'm saved."

"Yeah, I know who Jesus is."

"Sure, a personal relationship with Jesus would be cool, but He's dead isn't He?"

It was definitely a lot to process. I tried to speed up the interrogation: the questions, the responses, the reading of the floppy book, the "repeat this prayer after me," the closed eyes, the hugs, and the okay, I'm born again. I was just hoping they would wrap up the twenty questions so I wouldn't miss *All in the Family*.

It was the second time I was born again, so I was getting pretty good at it. The only difference was this time there was no Coke, cookies, or pictures of dead babies. I really can't remember how many times I was born again on the landing; I just knew I couldn't tell my dad; he didn't want those people in our house or anyone trying to change our religious beliefs from those being taught at Holy Cross.

The whole born-again/Jerry Falwell/Thomas Road/Liberty Baptist cloud hovered over Lynchburg, Virginia. The cloud could deliver gentle rain one day and acid rain the next. Jerry's army marched through Lynchburg converting people as if we were reliving the crusades. Salvation was the product of the day.

Even though my multiple salvation experiences never had a lasting impact for more than five minutes, they did open my eyes to what people were doing around me. I had a front-row seat to the Jesus revolution, and Jerry Falwell was the headliner, the lead crusader.

After a while I began to understand their strategy and accept it for what it was worth. Knocks on the door or getting cornered in a parking lot at the grocery store by Jerry's foot soldiers were commonplace occurrences and sometimes cause for a healthy debate.

Occasionally, there were attempts for winning sinners to Jerry's side that made me eerily uncomfortable. During my senior year of high school, Lauren, a bright, beautiful cheerleader, was riding in a jeep on the back roads of Forest, just outside of Lynchburg. Her jeep collided with another vehicle and Lauren didn't make it out alive. It was a horrible tragedy at all levels.

Her family was a member of Jerry's Thomas Road Baptist Church, where the funeral was held. Thomas Road was packed with heartbroken high school friends and sympathetic members of the church. It was standing room only to mourn the passing of a lovely and promising young lady.

Throughout the service a number of people spoke, reflecting on Lauren's brief life. Then Jerry took command of his pulpit. I couldn't believe my ears. He was doing it right there, at Lauren's funeral. He was orchestrating an altar call at Lauren's funeral! With heads bowed, he asked people to raise their hands and then come down front to accept the Lord at Lauren's *funeral*! He was asking people to say the sinner's prayer *at Lauren's funeral!* Any connection to Jerry's crusade that could have blossomed in my heart died. I was shocked and angry at Jerry's gall for taking the opportunity of a full house of mostly new faces in the pews to perform an altar call. It was appalling.

Jerry wrapped up his barrage by confirming that it's what Lauren would have wanted. I wondered if Jerry even knew Lauren, if he had ever even spoken to her during her short, fragile life. He may have executed his assault on the sinners in the cavernous sanctuary with good intentions, but it was dreadful timing for those grieving hearts sitting in the pews that afternoon; or at least that was my perception.

It wasn't until thirty years later that I realized the true gift Jerry had offered during Lauren's funeral. I had spent so many years diametrically opposed to Jerry's approach that I missed the beauty in the message. He simply wanted non-believers to be exposed to God's truth. The intent was perfect; at the time I just didn't agree with his approach. I can only hope that, one day, someone will accept Christ and turn their life around because I have lived . . . even at my funeral.

For my wonder years in Richland Hills, I grew in my understanding of racial and religious hatred and how extremists could make a person run from truth and reality. Extremists are not concerned about truth; they are only concerned about their extreme positions and converting everyone to their point of view.

I learned a lot in Richland Hills even though I didn't know I was learning at the time. I thought learning happened at Brookville Elementary School or at Holy Cross Catholic School, where my parents insisted I go for junior high. I thought learning took place at one of the nine schools in four states I attended from kindergarten through high school.

I didn't realize the real education was taking place on the landing.

A Ray of Light

I am a part of all that I have met.
—ALFRED, LORD TENNYSON[6]

THREE HIGH SCHOOLS IN THREE years. Virginia, Maryland, and back to Virginia.

The Mayflower Moving and Storage Company made a pretty good living from the Krcelic family over the years. Since my parents first broke out of Chicago and ventured to the territory of Alaska, we packed the dishes and furniture ten times. It was important for my parents to break the cycle of inner-city struggle and move their young family to a place of opportunity. The cycle could not be broken unless someone took the intentional step outside of the circle. That was Mom and Dad; the cycle was broken. Every move was for a better job, a better opportunity, a better life for our family. My father was driven to succeed in business but, more importantly, in earning his college degree. He knew that education was the key to a better life.

When he graduated from high school in Chicago, his mother didn't have the resources to send him to the University of Illinois for the year. Not to be discouraged, he enrolled at DeVry Technical College to earn his associates degree in electrical engineering. But that wasn't good enough; he knew a bachelor's degree would accelerate his advancement and opportunity in the workplace. My father moved us from frigid Alaska to sunny Florida in 1965 to take a job at NASA and work on the Apollo space missions. It was John F. Kennedy's vision to land a man on the moon and return him safely to earth, and my dad had a hand in the success of that mission. He also enrolled at the Florida Institute of Technology where he went to night school in quest of the invaluable bachelor's degree. During the day he was a 60-hour-a-week communications engineer on one of the most important projects in the history of mankind, and by night he was a 15-hour-a-week college student studying to earn his bachelor's degree and become the first Krcelic to ever graduate from college. I have never known a more dedicated and committed person—a man with a deep dedication to his work and a strong love for his family.

His commitment to education ultimately engaged all of my three siblings to follow suit. Bobby graduated from Virginia Tech then went on to be a colonel in the U.S. Army, Tammy from William & Mary who later went on to earn a Master's Degree, and Louie, the high school dropout, was the first Krcelic ever to earn a Master's Degree. Louie was a pure example of turning one's life around and overcoming horrible obstacles that can potentially ruin anyone's life. He was a role model. Dad had set the bar high.

Every move was an adventure. It wasn't dreaded because my mother made it exciting—a new place with new things to see, new things to do, and new people to meet. My first five years in school were at five different schools. Under ordinary circumstances and without a loving and caring mother, those moves would have been horrible. It didn't matter where we were moving; Mom made it something to look forward to, a thrilling journey to a new place. She always made it feel like a new adventure.

Just like any other family, there were always hard times and dysfunction; but there has always been a bond in our family that is only found pulsating through veins—a deep-rooted blood that ran proudly from the old country: Poland, Croatia, Hungary, and Czechoslovakia. There were problems, disagreements, and complaining, but the family always stayed together and made the best of the forecast on the horizon. Blood.

This type of commitment and bond also came from faith, a strong unquestioning Christian faith in Jesus Christ, although we never called ourselves Christians. Our faith was grown in the Catholic Church with a belief in God. That was about it. I didn't read the Bible, study the stories and characters in its pages, or concentrate much on Jesus Christ. That's not to say my parents or siblings didn't crack the pages of the big white Bible when I wasn't around; it just wasn't on my to-do list. Other than the scripture readings and the sermon during Sunday mass, for us Catholics it was pretty much the priest, the saints, the pope, and God, not necessarily in that order.

By the time I got to eleventh grade and my ninth school, moving was standard operating procedure. From ninth grade to eleventh grade we moved from Lynchburg to Rockville, Maryland, and back to Lynchburg. Unfortunately, we moved back to a different school district than before, which meant new friends again even though I was in my old stomping grounds. I pleaded with my parents to send me back to the high school I attended in ninth grade with my old friends, but the additional cost was way too much. Although I was back in Jerry's Lynchburg with friends throughout the city, I knew only one person at my new school. Three years of high school, three schools, three sets of new people. But it wasn't always a bad thing going to a new school; I usually became the quick interest of the single girls in class. New guy, no baggage.

All of the moves didn't afford the opportunity to get involved in youth groups or have any substantive church stability. The only stable constant was Mom and my sister, Tammy. Tammy treated me like I was her own. Even though we were five years apart, she always helped me with school and played games when no one else was around.

A few of my friends were members of church youth organizations. The groups were intriguing but nothing that was so interesting I was ready to join up and sing Christmas carols at retirement communities, something that was never on my to-do list either. On a steamy summer night in 1979 after driver's education training, I walked into the Big-T Burger across from Brookville High School with one of my friends who was taking the class with me. That changed everything; it wasn't the Big-T Burger, fries, and a Coke, but it was the dark-haired, brown-eyed girl serving it, Donna.

Donna was the first person that I really connected with in a way that made me forget myself. She made my heart race. Donna was ever so kind, soft-spoken, pretty, and gentle. It was an instant connection, at least on my part. Donna was a senior at the rival high school across the street, the same one Tammy graduated from and my brother Louie dropped out of during our prior stint in Lynchburg. I was a rising junior at the relatively new Jefferson Forest High. We had different sets of friends. I was a part-time Catholic and she was a full-fledged Southern Baptist with some sort of family connection to Jerry Falwell and the moral majority. She came from a broken family and lived with her grandparents in an old, small, white, wood-frame house.

I was now living in a very nice and very large house in Thomas Jefferson's Poplar Forest. Our home was a stone's throw from where Thomas Jefferson courted his slave mistress Sally Hemings. Everyone thought we were rich because of the size of our pillared, two-story colonial house. I really didn't think much of it; it was just another house. If we really were rich, I wouldn't have to still be mowing the lawn myself, much less with a push mower. Rich people either had someone else mow their grass or used a riding mower.

Donna's and my life were incredibly different, so opposite. The chance we would ever even go out on a date was remote. We talked for a moment and smiled. I got my order, and my friend and I would keep looking back at the counter from our vinyl-covered chairs to see if she was looking in our direction. It was like we were playing some high school game of "I hope she likes me." Well, we *were* in high school.

We left, but I had no idea as to the next time we might see each other again, if there would be a next time. The one thing that was certain was I couldn't get Donna out of my mind. I started dating another girl at her school who turned out to be her good friend. We would run into each other from time to time, but I was dating her friend. That didn't stop my attraction to Donna.

One day in August there was an early morning knock at the door while I was in a dead teen-age morning slumber. "Gene, there's someone at the door for you," my mom shouted.

I rolled out of bed and stumbled up the stairs to the front door wondering who in the world was at my house looking for me before 9:00 a.m. in the summer. It was Donna.

"Hey," she said with a smile. "Want to go for a ride? I have to run some errands for my dad." She was out running the errands for him while he was out of town. Donna didn't live with him now; he was living with his new family.

I wasn't looking my best this early in the morning, but why not? "Sure."

I offered to drive our brand new burgundy AMC Pacer but she opted for her dad's mint-condition red Ford Maverick. The journey began. I figured she must have liked me because why else is she knocking at my door when there's still dew on the grass?

Our differences didn't matter. We were two teenagers who liked each other. Romeo and Juliet weren't really concerned about life's differences; they were concerned about commonality . . . the commonality of the heart.

As our relationship grew, so did our like for each other. Our like turned to love, and love turned into the expectation that we were going to get married one day. Donna was a ray of light into my life. My strong dislike of anything Christian put my own convictions at odds. I didn't care about Catholic, I didn't care about Baptist, I didn't care about her parents' or grandparents' beliefs, I didn't care about my parents' beliefs. I was seventeen and I cared about her.

Donna was my first real love. We explored life as teenagers in love do and we became extremely close despite our religious beliefs. We spent as much time together as we could, which meant, for me, attending Christian youth activities through her church and high school. We drank warm apple cider at youth gatherings before we sang Christmas carols at retirement communities. I would hang out with her Christian friends and discover other activities I had never been exposed to before. There were no pictures of dead babies, and the youth groups were just normal high school kids having fun without alcohol or drugs. I liked it.

The ray of light cracked my perception of born-again Christians, and I gained an appreciation for a group of people I had grown wary of and been taught to dislike. My parents even liked Donna. They loved her kind and gentle nature and knew how I felt about her. She wasn't condemning of my Catholic faith; she was tolerant. As I learned about her, I learned about me. I opened up to possibilities that were alien to me. She helped round the edges of my wandering faith.

The only Bible I had known, other than the big, white family-tree Bible, were those stuffed in the church pews. When Donna gave me my first Bible as a no-special-occasion gift, I was taken aback. It was a green, hard-backed, leather edition with "The Living Bible" emblazoned across the front. In the bottom right corner was my name in gold lettering. I really didn't know what to think of this sacred book other than, *Wow, what am I supposed to do with this?*

On the inside front cover it read, "Gene, I hope this Bible will become a very important part of your life as you learn to understand the world and that you will establish a closer relationship with Christ. I love you and I will help you in any way that I can. Forever, Donna." The words were prophetic, although not for another twenty-plus years. At the time, I couldn't quite understand what "a closer relationship with Christ" meant. It was difficult to wrap my head around having a relationship with a man who died two thousand years ago. He wasn't someone I could see or talk to; that's what the priest was for—to help me understand the mysteries of God.

Donna encouraged me to write in the Bible like all of the other floppy editions I saw in Richland Hills or the one she read from. But it was the Holy Bible, not something to be defiled by writing in or highlighting. Her gift, although much appreciated, remained dormant other than when she encouraged us to read it together. I was in love and she was my girlfriend. If she wanted me to read it with her, I read it. But that was the extent of it. There was no extra-curricular reading in the green leather book for me although she gave me verses to read from in Matthew, Deuteronomy, Leviticus, and Hebrews. Even the little pamphlet with quotes from Romans on purity and Philippians on doing all things through Christ had no effect on my study plans or my teenage tendencies.

Other than the sparse, lightly underlined choice verses, only part of 1 Corinthians 7 was boldly underlined in red felt-tip ink: "And if a Christian woman has a husband who isn't a Christian, and he wants her to stay with him, she must not leave him. For perhaps the husband who isn't a Christian may become a Christian with the help of his Christian wife." So I surmised the would-be non-Christian husband was me and the would-be Christian wife was her. *That's right . . . I'm Catholic, not Christian,* I realized. She was Baptist . . . a Christian.

Of course, dating Donna offered many other opportunities to say the sinner's prayer and offer myself to Christ once again, and again and again. I thought you were supposed to accept Jesus Christ as your Savior only once. In my case, I had to start counting using both hands and one of my feet. Every time I was led through the process, I questioned my position with God, so I would say the grace-filled prayer over and over.

As high school wrapped up, Donna ended up at a small college in Virginia, and I ventured to Chapel Hill and the University of North Carolina a year later. Our paths eventually diverged during my sophomore year at UNC despite various attempts at trying to make it work. College was next, girlfriend or no girlfriend; college and all of her distractions would be my true love for the next few years.

The words Donna underlined in my green Bible, 1 Corinthians 7:13–14, would hold true. I was a non-Christian and the relationship with my future Christian wife would be the key to my salvation. In due time, the prophetic verses would reveal their truth, but with Mary Fields, not Donna.

Chapel Hill, Y'all

We are the champions
We are the champions
No time for losers
'Cause we are the champions of the world.
—FREDDY MERCURY[7]

RED HAIR, FRECKLES, AND A born-again Christian. No matter where I turned, my destiny was to be in close relationship with a born-again Christian.

Robert Carlton Rogers III had a phenomenal physique and was a superstar at any sport he chose to lend his natural skill to. I spoke with him a couple of times from Lynchburg to Raleigh on the phone but we never met face to freckle until August 1981. We would spend the next year together in room 421 at Ehringhaus dormitory overlooking Boshamer baseball stadium. Ehringhaus was the dormitory where the football players lived. It was easy access to the exclusive athlete-only dining facility located in the basement of the dorm.

Our outlooks on life and college couldn't have been more divergent on the polar opposite scale. Rob was born again and I was born to party. Rob came prepared to study and attempt to walk on as a North Carolina Tar Heel football player. I came prepared to drink in all that college life had to offer, as evidenced by my amply stocked liquor shelf. It soon became an empty liquor shelf after I spent the night naked on the suite bathroom floor surrounded by my own vomit. The next morning I begged Rob to pour all of my liquor down the drain because I swore I would never drink again. He gladly obliged, much to my future dismay. I cussed like a sailor and I don't recall Rob ever uttering a swear word. He was relatively quiet and I tended to be loud and boisterous at times. We were worlds apart. But he had a humble confidence and calm about him. It was something I yearned for but had no idea what it was or how to get it.

Our primary commonality was music. Rob owned a wide assortment of funk and R&B cassettes. It was much to my pleasure as rap was being birthed onto the musical landscape. The Bar-Kays, Gap Band, Brick, Earth, Wind & Fire, Sugar Hill Gang, and Grandmaster Flash were only one button away from bumping room 421. As a Christian, Rob was solid, much like my steady girlfriend, Donna. I thought I was getting away from consistent Christian influence, but God's plan was different from my own.

Our suite-style dorm was shared with three other rooms. In one room across the hall were two freshmen of African American decent whose sleeping quarters always smelled like a fresh pine forest after a spring rain. The room next to ours was registered to two upper-class All-American football players who may have slept in their on-campus housing one night out of the semester. It was a shame because it was the only room in the suite that had an air conditioner. The fourth room diagonally across from ours was the home to two junior transfers, one from Bangladesh and his roommate, Scott. Scott, an aspiring sports columnist, was a junior transfer from the University of Connecticut majoring in English. He looked like he had stepped off of any college campus from the 1960s. He was clean cut, khaki-clad, with short blonde hair and a personality to match mine. We had so much in common. Not only did we both have Polish ancestors, we also both loved sports and were Catholic.

After I moved into the dorm, my parents pulled out of Chapel Hill and back to Lynchburg. I was left in the southern part of heaven with a Christian roommate, a Catholic suitemate, and a stocked liquor shelf. Scott and I soon found ourselves sitting at "the pit" in the middle of campus with a cold 12-pack of Michelob from the Happy Store singing the lyrics to Rick James's "Super Freak." I thought, *I can get used to college life in no time.* That sunny summer Carolina afternoon was the first day away from home for the rest of my life. It was as exhilarating as sitting on an icy mountain top eating a York Peppermint Patty.

As a teenager, the first day on your college campus is the experience of a lifetime and a rite of passage, but for my mother, it was melancholy, as I was the fourth of four children to leave the nest. Mom would now be home alone for much of the time as my father traveled overseas developing global telephone technology for GTE and the airline industry. But I was finally free.

I knew my parents hoped I would go to mass at college, so Scott and I attended the local Chapel Hill Catholic Church. The only thing memorable about the service on my first Sunday in the Hill was the picnic in the parking lot afterward. The church grilled hot dogs and served ice-cold Budweiser from trash cans. Now that was the kind of church I liked. Feed your soul, feed your stomach, and feed your buzz. The next Sunday, there were no hot dogs and no ice-cold Budweiser, just your standard Catholic mass. That was the last time I went to church in college, other than the one hell-fire and brimstone service I attended with Rob at the Baptist church across from the Happy Store. Church just wasn't my thing.

I had left a small high school where I was a part of the in-crowd. I was a big fish and fairly popular in a small pond of 700 students. I started on a district and regional championship football team, won countless public speaking awards, was in the National Honor Society, and was the star of the school plays. Now, in Chapel Hill, I was just a regular small fish in a sea of 22,000 students. But not for long.

As fate painted its portrait of life, I stumbled across a sign on campus that had a picture of a microphone on it, and the sign read "Mic-Man Tryouts." I had no idea what a mic-man was, but if it had to do with talking on a microphone in front of people, it had my name written all over it. I couldn't think of any better way to meet girls, even though I had a girlfriend a few hours away in Virginia. The tryouts were for the mic-man at the home football games, a position held by a student to lead the cheerleaders and student body at game time. It made no difference to me that I had never been to a major college football game before, or that the responsibilities were leading a student body dominated by condescending upperclassmen.

Earlier that day I had met All-American basketball player James Worthy and his girlfriend. She also lived in Ehringhaus and was a senior varsity cheerleader. She taught me a few Carolina cheers and gave me an idea of what it's like on the sidelines in front of 50,000 screaming fans. At the tryouts, each would-be mic-man had five minutes to woo the judges and the crowd of spectators. After the dozen contestants shucked and jived through a routine, the judges named the new vocal leader for UNC football games. I was the first freshman mic-man in the school's long history of mic-men. It would be a year where UNC garnered significant national attention as it vaulted to #3 in the national college football polls, and the student body would be led by a newcomer . . . a freshman. The result of the tryouts was an outcome many upperclassmen didn't take too well.

"Freshman! How can a freshman be mic-man?" I overheard as an upperclassman walked by me at my first game. "He knows nothing about our tradition!"

The Daily Tar Heel, the college newspaper, featured a headline front-page article with my picture circulating my story throughout the student body. Letters to the editor and editorials were written accompanied by full caricatures. Some of it was good press; some of it was bad press. But when you are trying to make a name for yourself on a liberal arts campus of 20,000+ students, no press is bad press, especially if your goal is to meet the female variety of co-ed. In the same year, I was cast as the lead in two plays for the Theatre Department, and everything filled my ego like a balloon thirsty for air.

Although Donna was trying to make our relationship work, my new-found popularity and ego would have no part in a faithful relationship. What she couldn't see or hear didn't happen as far as I was concerned. I was well known and getting drunk off the cup of college life. I got a B+ on my first college test, I had girls I didn't know leaving me notes on my door, I had access—I could do no wrong! The big fish from a small pond was now a big fish in a big sea.

But no matter how big I thought I was, on a campus like UNC, there were always bigger fish . . . like the Michael Jordan fish. As runner up to Buzz Peterson for North Carolina high school player of the year, Michael Jordan was just trying to find his place. And he did. In April of 1982 at the national championship game in New Orleans, the Wilmington native hit the winning shot over Patrick Ewing's Georgetown Hoyas to clinch the National Championship for the Tar Heels. Franklin Street broke out in a frenzy as we emptied out of dorm rooms, bars, and restaurants and partied in the street throughout the night. Rob and I finally rolled back to the dorm after the morning sun had already risen; class was optional on Tuesday. Freshman year was good, very good!

First semester freshman year was too good. After a stellar D average at Christmas break, my father made it abundantly clear that

my average after year one would be a B or I would be enrolling at
Central Virginia Community College in Lynchburg, right down
the road from Liberty Baptist College. If only I had listened to my
father when I was signing up for classes; he told me to take Spanish,
and I took German. I failed German. Second semester I listened
to my father, and I took Spanish. I earned a B+. Father usually did
know best. My grades rallied and Chapel Hill remained home for
the remainder of college.

The roller coaster of freshman year wouldn't be the same without
being saved . . . again. My oldest brother Bobby was an officer in
the U.S. Army stationed in Germany. One afternoon I received a
call in the dorm, and my mother was on the phone in tears.

"Your brother Bobby was in a car accident," she said with a
cracked voice. "He's in serious condition, and it looks like he will
be in a full body cast for a long time. I think he broke his back."
He was driving his new forest green BMW on the Autobahn at a
high rate of speed and hit a patch of black ice, totaling his car and
leaving him in a life-threatening situation.

Bobby and I were ten years apart, which meant for most of my
memory he was hanging out with his teenage friends and didn't
want to be bothered by his baby brother. By the time I was eight,
he was off to college at Virginia Tech. But he was my big brother,
so I had a deep love for him. After the call from my mother, Rob
and I prayed together. He asked me if I wanted to ask God for His
love and if I would accept His Son Jesus Christ as my Savior. I was
scared for Bobby, and I would do anything if it would help save my
brother's life. I was desperate for help, not just for my brother, but
I knew I needed help. I wanted what Rob had; I just didn't know
how to get it. I asked Christ to be my Savior, my Healer. Unlike all
of the other times before, this time I felt a little different. It wasn't a
big bang revelation; it was slight, subtle . . . but it was different.

Bobby healed over time as I was on a path of healing as well. He took mere months to recover, while correcting the true condition of my heart would take decades. Rob helped continue the process that Donna had begun. He was also there to help me through the pain after another traumatic phone call from a friend notified me that an old girlfriend had been killed by a drunk driver. She was walking her dog when a repeat offender crested a hill and swerved off the road, killing her and her dog instantly. The pain was something I had a hard time dealing with by myself. Rob was there to help ease the pain and reveal light. He was a calming force, an anchor.

Through my antics and occasionally absurd behavior, Rob was always steady. When I stretched beyond safe boundaries, he was there to pull me to safety. Being around him helped tame my tongue, and I learned behaviors I needed. Rob was a rock. He always had fun without drinking, drugs, or being vulgar. He was everything good about a college student. He studied hard, played hard, and prayed hard. He worked his way onto the varsity football team and earned the starting kicker's position his sophomore year, along with a 53-yard field goal against Pitt and Dan Marino on ABC's Monday Night College Football. Rob was a true role model.

Even though we did not room together after freshman year or really spend any meaningful time together since, he helped shape my faith in a way that would last a lifetime. It was odd that I would spend my life envying certain people, certain Christians. My stereotypical view of Christians was unfairly colored by Bible-thumping extremists that preached hate instead of love. If I was truly honest with myself, I would have to say that for most of my life I was agnostic. I hoped and wanted to believe there was a Savior named Jesus and that His Father was *the* supreme God, but my need for tangible proof kept me from living a life of faith. If my faith in God was a balloon, it was empty. Rob at least opened my eyes and showed me there was a balloon, and it took work to fill it. My edges were rounded once again.

Ego Is Me

I fed my ego, but not my soul.
—YAKOV SMIRNOFF[8]

MY FAITH BALLOON WAS NEAR empty and my ego balloon was stretched beyond capacity!

Sophomore year dealt a critical blow to everything I thought I had achieved as a freshman. What I had known as starring roles in my extra-curricular activities were things of the past. Instead of automatically retaining the position of mic-man, annual auditions were held for the coveted job. *I have the experience now*, I thought. *Winning it again should be no problem!*

As with any incumbent, complacency is not your friend. Since I reigned for an entire year, my ego kept me blinded to the reality that someone could actually beat me at a performance competition. I auditioned. I did not commit to my best. I was complacent. I lost.

The loss was a cruel blow to my ego and who I thought I was, Mr. Invincible. It served as a sign of things to come. As an editorial had stated after I won as a freshman, if I maintained the position for four years, I would become a Carolina tradition. No one had ever been a mic-man for four or five years in a row. I shouldn't have read my own press clippings. I knew I would win, hands down. I was complacent and I lost.

Throughout my sophomore year, I was my own worst enemy. With two starring roles in theatre productions a year earlier, I figured the roles would only become better and more frequent. Fate continued to paint its canvas, and I wasn't cast in another play during my five years as a UNC student. During my last two years at Chapel Hill, my concentration turned to journalism. With the reality of my own performance mediocrity stabbing me in the back, I declared a double major, adding Journalism to the Dramatic Arts degree. Writing and broadcast studies occupied my time, not stage performance. At least a career in writing or broadcasting added some substance to a post-graduate career.

Eric was a keenly focused student and ultra-serious about all of his endeavors. As second-year roommates go, he was a good guy and a solid person, but he wasn't Rob. I had less in common with him than with Rob, so I ended up hanging out with most of the freshmen on the fourth floor hall of Winston dorm. It meant less studying and more partying. A couple of my hall mates fell victim to an abundance of partying and ended up spending the rest of their college career at home or working as bag boys at the local Piggly Wiggly. Winston dorm was right across the street from Carmichael Auditorium, where the national champions played. Our dorm was the closest on-campus housing to the reigning cathedral of college basketball.

I had a new set of friends and built some lasting relationships, but I lacked any relationship with God. The truest connection I had with God started with Donna, and I was well on the way to destroying that. I had met another girl at UNC through the cousin of one of the cheerleaders. We started dating, exclusively. The fatal flaw in the relationship was that I was also dating Donna, exclusively. Neither relationship ever had a chance. Had I converted to the Church of Latter Day Saints and studied the Mormon teaching of Brigham Young, I would have been fine. Delusional behavior can only be recognized by those around the one afflicted, and only a true friend would try to halt the harmful behavior instead of encouraging it. I convinced myself I could maintain two separate worlds, two separate lives, one in Chapel Hill and the other in Farmville, Virginia. It was a charmed-horrible situation, a battle of right and wrong. According to me I was right; according to basic gentlemanly respect and honor, I was wrong. Rob wasn't there to snap me out of it and tell me that I was an idiot for such behavior.

My eyes were so covered with scales; truth and light were only figments of my imagination. The charade I was orchestrating across two states inevitably crashed down on me like a bursting levee behind hurricane-force winds. When Donna found out about my Chapel Hill girlfriend, both relationships unraveled. A life of abundance a year earlier was boldly met by a wasteland of personal malfunction. There was no one to blame for my failures but me. I was lost and I felt alone. My hall mates in Winston were great friends and fun to party with, but the stability in my life was gone. Donna was gone, Rob was gone. For the first time in years, there were no born-again Christians around me trying to save my soul and coerce me into reciting the sinner's prayer. There were no floppy Bibles. The freedom was liberating, but with that freedom I drifted away from God and any true understanding of His plan.

Donna emerged again out of the blue after we had been broken up for some time. She drove to my apartment, unannounced, during my junior year. We weren't dating and really had had no contact for months. She was in tears. She confessed to screwing up our relationship, which was actually mutual in a number of ways.

"If I move to Chapel Hill, do you think we can have a chance of getting back together?" she asked.

"Wow, I don't know." I was nearly speechless.

We talked for two days without any resolution to the proposition. I was confused, torn.

She drove back to Virginia and that was that. No reunification. It was truly over.

: : : : : :

I was drowning, I just didn't know it. I constantly found myself in circumstances that I now know could have easily pulled me down a one-way path with no hope of return.

And then it happened. After returning for my fourth year, or my first senior year as I called it, it happened. It started as an innocent conversation, a boy trying to talk a girl into going out for dinner while we were hanging out by the apartment complex pool. It would be a challenge to persuade Mary, a casual friend, to actually go out on a date. I had been working, building swimming pools in New Jersey all summer, and was ready to hang out with a real Carolina girl. She was complaining about her boyfriend at home who wasn't being romantic enough for her, and I was without constraint and looking for a date. She opened the door and I stuck my Converse All-Star in the gap before she could close it.

"Well, I know if you were my girlfriend, I would be romantic," I smoothed like a clown delivering the lamest pre-proposition ever. "Do you want to go out and have a drink somewhere tonight?"

She looked shocked. A bit hesitant.

"I guess so," she answered in an I'm-not-sure-if-I-really-want-to-go-out-with-you-or-not kind of way. "Sure."

"So, yes?"

"Yes."

"Great, I'll come get you at seven."

We ended up at Eliot's Nest to check out the legendary Doug Clark and the Hot Nuts. We were both laughing and having a great time, just friends amongst friends. A few fast dances, then Doug slowed it down, old school.

Awkward.

We were acquaintances and casual friends at best. Friends at our level didn't slow dance. We stood there and looked at each other sheepishly. *Why not?*

"You want to dance?" I eased, like *what else are we going to do?*

"Sure," Mary said a bit more confidently than I asked.

We danced. That was it.

I had never felt this odd attraction in an instant. It wasn't as if I had never felt an attraction to her, but she was more like a sister, just a friend. Mary wasn't in my plan for the rest of my life, and I would have bet my Datsun King Cab pickup truck I wasn't in hers either, but there was an oddly powerful attraction.

At that point I had no idea of her religious upbringing, her view on the Moral Majority, her political stance, whether or not she really liked college basketball, how extensive her album collection was, if she played Frisbee golf, or anything of real substance. It didn't make any difference. She was a pretty Carolina girl with a sweet southern accent that just stopped the world from spinning. My heart raced in a way it never had before. Everything about the moment was unexpected. It was perfect. I felt it, but did Mary?

At the moment you fall in love, you know. I knew. I was in love.

Fortunately, I could tell the chemistry wasn't just a bad experiment in a laboratory. It was a mutual attraction. But perhaps in the light of the next day, the feelings would fade and I would be back to my daily routine. Not the case. I couldn't get Mary out of my mind, and later I found out the same was true for her thoughts.

Since our apartment buildings were right next door to each other, we saw a lot of each other over the next two years. We were exclusive. She was my girlfriend. We learned everything about each other, spending as much time together as we could.

At the start of our relationship, Donna called. She had moved to Chapel Hill to earn an additional degree at UNC. Her apartment complex was only a few hundred yards away. She acted like she wanted to get together. I asked to see her, so she openly invited me to her apartment. She didn't tell me her new boyfriend was going to be sitting on the couch when I dropped by. I had no intent of smoothing out another proposition like the pool-side date. I wanted to see a friend who had meant so much to me in the past.

Donna seemed sad but uniquely happy. She was planning on getting married to her new boyfriend. Although I thought jealousy would have been the blue plate special, I was actually happy for her. I wanted for her to find someone that truly made her happy and matched her own Christian ideals.

My Christian identity was still unformed, but it turned out Mary's Christianity was solid. She had grown up in the Methodist church and did all the things kids in Christian youth ministry do. They learn the Bible and form an understanding of life based on Jesus Christ. But Mary was a different Christian. She didn't bludgeon me with the Bible or try to save me by reciting a prayer. She seemed normal to me. She had values, she had faith, and she was a Christian.

Growing up in a separated Christian family, her father was Catholic and devoutly attended mass every Saturday night while she and her mother went to the Methodist service on Sunday morning. It was a spiritually divided family. Mary gained a quiet but solid faith and belief in Jesus.

We never went to church together; instead we would picnic or canoe on Sundays. We'd go eat breakfast on Sunday mornings and then try to study as the morning would turn to afternoon and afternoon blended into Sunday night.

When graduation rolled around in the late spring of 1986, we knew it was only a matter of time until we'd be standing at the altar of her Methodist church, a Catholic marrying a Protestant, southern Christian. I only hoped it would be after a successful job offer in New York City.

In October of 1987, a year and a half after graduation, we were married with both a Catholic priest and a Methodist minister presiding over the ceremony. Ironically enough, her minister looked like a shorter version of Jerry Falwell. It was surreal, as every marriage is.

Our marriage started without our own church. She wasn't going to go to a Catholic church and I certainly wasn't going to go to a Methodist church. So we didn't go to church. She was a Christian and I was an agnostic at best, but we had each other.

As much as I loathed the moniker of *Christian*, I was married to one. We were tied at the hip, on paper and in person. I had married what I had tried to run away from all of my life. I had married a Christian.

Where Do We Go from Here?

We don't live here, we only work here.
—STEVE BIONDO[9]

TWENTY-FOUR YEARS OLD, MARRIED, AND living in the Greenville-Spartanburg region of South Carolina. I was in the buckle of the Bible belt. If Spartanburg, South Carolina, wasn't technically the buckle, it was certainly one of the holes on the belt. It was a sleepy southern town, home to the Hardee's hamburger chain, nestled in the shadow of emerging Greenville. Greenville, South Carolina, was home to the extremely conservative and ultra right-wing Bob Jones University. The university's founder, Bob Jones, reportedly "called the pope the anti-Christ and dismissed Catholicism as a 'Satanic counterfeit'"; he allegedly said, "I would rather see a saloon on every corner than a Catholic in the White House."[10] And following the death of Pope Paul VI in 1978, Bob Jones Jr. supposedly called him the "archpriest of Satan, a deceiver, and he has, like Judas, gone to his own place."[11] And I thought Jerry Falwell wielded the heavy hand of judgmental Christian conservatism.

As irony would reverse her path, later in business I developed a partnership with Bob Jones University that was a loving and caring outreach to an atheistic community from China. My perception of the Bob Jones family softened over the years as I was able to personally feel their true Christian love.

South Carolina was never in my plan for a career and raising a family; it was a state I never considered . . . I wasn't even sure if they had running water. I had always envisioned living in New York City after college, not born-again Christian land. My vision was to work in a big city, make a mountain of cash, and retire by the time I was fifty. Since my first job offer came in the form of a television position in Spartanburg, then Spartanburg it was. God's plan was being revealed; my plan was nowhere to be found.

One of the standard questions in the South when you meet someone is, "Where do you go to church?" Mary and I didn't attend church. My job required substantial weekend work at the TV station, and if there was an occasional Sunday off, I rested. Resting on Sunday was one of the few biblical principles by which I lived and it certainly didn't entail having to get up early and go to church. We didn't talk about going to church, we didn't look for a church, and it really didn't matter to me. Perhaps it was because Mary wasn't interested in going to a Catholic church and I definitely wasn't going to any Methodist church, so we opted out.

A strong relationship with God and a spiritual support group would have come in handy as Mary and I soul-searched about my taking a job with a small startup company in Greenville. I would be running a newly formed media company and have an ownership stake in the venture. I had the confidence that I could be a successful entrepreneur, but I was without any practical business knowledge. There was no thriving Internet to teach me how to build a company in five easy steps. We felt compelled to take the risk, sell the house, and relocate twenty miles down the road. We had no real community or church ties to Spartanburg, so the moving part was easy.

Church and a community of faith only became an issue after we moved to Greenville when God bestowed the blessing upon us of parents-to-be. We had to start looking for a place to worship so our child could be baptized. Even though we disagreed on how and where to worship, not baptizing our child was not an option.

We searched.

We visited.

Methodist, no. Catholic, no. Baptist was out of the question! Lutheran, too much like Catholic. Episcopal, too much like Catholic. Church of God, are you kidding me? Presbyterian, hmm.

Saint Andrews Presbyterian Church was a little more formal than Methodist and a little less formal than Catholic. It was middle ground, the perfect solution in the faith negotiation. We finally joined Saint Andrews, but even though I officially became a Presbyterian in 1991, I was still a Catholic. Once a Catholic, always a Catholic, or in my case, an agnostic Catholic.

We participated in worship service, joined a Sunday school class, and were even recruited to teach a "hot-topic" young adult class. I was in no way qualified to teach a Sunday school class; however, I was the perfect antagonist for a weekly discussion on divisive issues and how we as members of the church body should deal with those issues. At twenty-eight, I had no biblical understanding and thus no qualifications to teach in church. But the congregation was small and willing instructors were at a minimum.

: : : : : :

The birth of a child changed everything.

Caroline was born on January 22, 1992. Childbirth is a miracle, a beautiful supernatural gift from God. Seeing the top of Caroline's head for the first time as Mary gave birth was the single most important and extraordinary moment of my life. She was mine. Mary and I created her in our image—our child.

Caroline was not only ours, she was God's—God's child, made in His image.

Even though we were not faithful churchgoers, I needed to start taking church a little more seriously. It was abundantly clear that our child, and hopefully children, were going to be raised with church influence, not a split denomination household like Mary's family, and not a transient, part-time church-going crew like mine. We would raise our children in the church, together. Denominational compromise was the first step.

Step two required faithful attendance. Step two was more challenging. Caroline was still too young for substantial learning opportunities, and sleeping in with a child was always a gift on any day of the week, especially the weekend. So we were part time.

Then came our second child, Alexis, three years later. Her birth was as equally important and miraculous as Caroline's. My fear was that I wouldn't be able to love a second child as much as the first. *How can I create more love for a child?* I thought. *I'm already giving Caroline all the love a parent can give; it was all I have. Can love just grow? Can a person simply create more love?*

Yes!

The love for Alexis was equally as great, no different than the equal love God has for every new child. It was simple to grasp the intensity and fathomless love a person can have for one of their own. It's the same fathomless love God holds for us.

:::::

With two young children, our house that was perfect for a young couple all of a sudden got real small. When I was on a business trip to China, Mary was on a quest to find the perfect house in the perfect school district. While I was eating sticky white rice and drinking snake blood, Mary put a down payment on a lot on the other side of Greenville in the thriving metropolis of Powdersville, where one of the best school districts in the state was located. We wanted to make sure the next move secured a local school district with an excellent academic reputation.

There were only two problems: the new home would be quite a distance from our church, and we began building the new house without selling the old one. After multiple months of dual house payments, living beyond our means, and arguments about money and our decision to jump in feet-first with the new build, the stress was at a climax! In desperation, my mother told me to dig a hole in the front yard, plant a Saint Joseph upside down facing away from the house, and say a big prayer. It was an old Catholic remedy for quickly selling a house. It sounded like some Catholic voodoo, but we were desperate and ready to try anything. It's not like Walmart had a random Joseph for sale by the shampoo and toothpaste aisle, so we borrowed him from our Christmas manger scene we dutifully admired every year.

Two months later the house sold. We thought it would have been a matter of days, but upside-down Saint Joseph had another plan.

Before we moved, I dug where I thought Joseph was buried so I could reacquaint him with his wife and so Mother Mary wouldn't have to look after baby Jesus solo. Saint Joseph was nowhere to be found. I was searching in an empty tomb. I dug in another spot— no Joseph. I finally gave up the archaeological dig, without Saint Joseph. To this day, the Krcelic family nativity scene has a devout shepherd looking over baby Jesus with Saint Mary.

With one problem solved, our focus turned to finding a new church home, one closer to our house. We searched for a new church with a thriving youth program where our girls would grow up, get confirmed, graduate, and one day get married. The quest for a new church home was a journey of love, one for our daughters, not knowingly for me.

At the suggestion of a friend and coworker, we visited her place of worship, Fourth Presbyterian Church. It was a relatively small church where the 800+ member congregation worshiped in the ninety-year-old stone building behind large red doors. Inside the sanctuary, its off-white walls were accented by beautifully descriptive stained glass windows representing God from Abraham to the resurrection above the red carpeted floor. It was beautiful, solemn, and spectacular in its quaint, simple splendor. There was no crucifix of Jesus hanging from the ceiling like in most Catholic churches; there was only a simple two-foot-high gold cross situated at the center of the communion table.

The person offering the message that day was the young associate pastor with a commanding presence and a direct simplicity to his theological delivery, Reverend Todd Speed. He was excellent, a modern-day Father Ron without the required collar. As we left the wooden-pewed sanctuary, he stood at the bottom of the stairs next to the bronze rail.

"Gene, welcome," Todd greeted me to my astonishment.

I checked to make sure it wasn't nametag Sunday as I glanced at my shirt. That he knew my name struck me cold. It was clear. Fourth Presbyterian would become our new church home.

I often hear people discuss the topic of knowing. "How do you know the answer to God's plan? How do you know when God reveals the answer to a prayer? How do you know when God speaks to you?"

The years have revealed to me that you know when you know. When the answer is abundantly clear, you feel it inside your heart. You just know!

The answer for our family was clear when we left the small stone church that glorious Sunday afternoon. We just knew!

Bible for Dummies

"Ask and it will be given to you;
seek and you will find;
knock and the door will be opened to you.
For everyone who asks receives;
the one who seeks finds;
and to the one who knocks,
the door will be opened."
—MATTHEW 7:7–8 (NIV)

FOURTH PRESBYTERIAN CHURCH SEEMED PERFECT.
They were blessed with an active young adult group and a vibrant
youth program, which was critical for our children. We were the
new faces in the crowd, so we were still outsiders trying to learn
the ropes of a coat-and-tie-clad congregation. I was a rebel—no
coat and tie for me. They were lucky to get a sweater vest. Our
prior church was dress down every week, because God loved us
the same regardless of what we wore on Sunday. Right? I wanted
to dress nice, but on Sunday I was business casual at best. I refused
to conform to the unwritten dress code and style standards of the
new church; after all, I was still a Catholic at heart. I simply wanted
to attend worship, go to Sunday school, and check out the various
activities of the church. Becoming a part of the religious church
machine was not an option—don't ask me to be a deacon, and
there was no chance the church administration was going to ask

me to be an elder. I just wanted to settle in nice and quietly as a face in the pews.

I was easing into understanding a new faith community and I felt like a first grader; unfortunately Sunday school was a college-level curriculum. The rest of the congregation was studying at an advanced pace and I was at a remedial level. I felt lost.

A typical Sunday school went like this: "You know the story of Joseph and the coat of many colors. Let's explore . . ."

That's where I tuned out or got left behind in the balance of the meaningful discussion. Growing up in our traveling Catholic church family, there was never any Bible exploration. A gaping hole was where my basic Bible 101 should have been. After a few weeks I had to speak up or get left totally behind.

"You know the story of Jesus and the rich man. Let's explore . . ."

"Ah, excuse me," I'd blurt with little reservation. "Can we review that please? I'm really not too familiar with that particular story."

I was hungry for biblical knowledge, not having had any foundation in the past, and I didn't want to get left behind in my quest for the truth of Scripture. My week had no room for extracurricular Bible research, so it was now or never.

I began to learn, but my thirst was never quenched. I was a biblical infant in the body of a grown man.

The young adult groups were pivotal for my growth and understanding. I quizzed my church friends and absorbed their perspectives on faith and Jesus as mine was forming like an embryo in a womb. As I was nurtured, I grew. As I asked basic questions, the foundation of my faith was gaining proper footings. My thirst grew to a ravenous hunger, often bringing me to throw out outrageous questions such as, "Well, why can't we merge evolution and creation? Is it so crazy to think that Adam and Eve could have possibly been fish? . . . Wouldn't it be even more poignant if the stone wasn't rolled away from Jesus' tomb, and He was missing with the stone intact when they came to prepare His body? . . . Come on now, do you really think Mary was a virgin? . . . What difference does it make if Jesus was married to Mary Magdalene?"

Then the practical, rational me would emerge. "The Roman tomb guards were probably on the take and let the body be removed, or they fell asleep and Jesus' disciples stole His body."

It was a constant ebb and flow of belief and doubt, truth and fiction, faith and lack thereof. Digging in the minds and hearts of my peers even deeper, I found many of their doubts were no different than mine. Rationalizing the words in the Bible with my skeptical nature was standard operating procedure for this growing Christian. That's simply how I rolled. But I just couldn't take the leap of faith and accept the Bible as written.

Picking up the church Bible lingo wasn't that difficult. My questions started to round at the edges and my comments started to make better sense in the class. It appeared that I was figuring it out; I started to sound like I knew what I was talking about . . . but still that treacherous leap of faith was before me. It wasn't that I was fearful of it; I just didn't know how to take the leap. I had been training, but I was still not completely prepared.

On the outside and through my words and kind deeds, others saw a strong Christian church member, while my heart was still lost, still doubting, still crying out for the truth. The leap of faith was too great. I was searching for the missing link, the elusive piece of fact that would complete my transformation. My heart was still lost.

I attended church on Sunday, went to Sunday school, religiously took part in Wednesday night supper, and volunteered when asked. I rarely said "no" to the leaders of the church. I was growing but was no candidate for any leadership role in the church.

: : : : : :

My church community lit the flame, but it was still dim. I needed more. I wanted an open, free-flowing, cutting-edge dialogue where I could explore outrageous perspectives but still have a level of theological direction and accuracy.

Dan was an investor in my new company. He was a regular guy with all the stresses of success, business, and family. His company was doing quite well, and from my perspective he was a role model for all things good and successful. Dan had it all. Even beyond his normal struggles and victories there was something special about him. He was at peace. He would inject his faith and commitment to God into casual conversations. It was just enough for me to take the bait. A part of me wanted to be like him.

His financial success wasn't what drew me to him; it was his peace and talk of God that drew me in like a moth to a flame. He was a normal guy, one of the boys, and didn't have a glazed, brainwashed look to his gaze.

He mentioned an experience when he woke up in the middle of the night, something he rarely did, and God showed him the solution to a problem that he was unable to solve by himself. Dan spoke of people and businesses being ordained by God and about the greater purpose we are all called to follow.

It all sounded rational and reasonable. God sounded normal, not like some intangible concept living above the clouds with an army of winged angels. Dan helped make believing in God and the wonders of Jesus a tangible reality.

Although the church was helping pour the cement of my foundation, Dan was the curing element my faith so desperately needed.

I asked him if he would engage in a Bible study with me and with anyone else who wanted to join. He knew the kind of radical group I was hoping to create. He agreed, with the provision that David Martin, a leader of a businessman's ministry, would lead the study. David was the ringer. Dan delivered a sound message but David took it to another level of conscious reality. He was so well-equipped at letting every conversation rage in any given direction then bringing it all back to absolute biblical understanding and truth in a free-flowing motion. David was a humble expert at his calling.

Our Bible study included a wide range of thoughts, perspectives, and faiths: Protestants, Catholics, atheists, agnostics, an occasional Jew, and an infrequent Buddhist were all participating in the discussion. We were attorneys, business owners, employees, unemployed, salesmen, music producers, musicians, and whoever else wanted to challenge or learn about the existence of God in our everyday lives and eternal future. It wasn't your everyday run-of-the-mill Bible study. It was edgy, provocative, unsettling, argumentative, and sometimes awkward. We discussed spiritual warfare and the spiritual plane of existence that good and evil battle on for one's soul. We discussed that being on Satan's radar was a good thing, for those who are not on his radar are already confined within his grasp. Those who have extreme potential to live out God's gracious plan for their lives and the lives of others are the very ones who threaten Satan's power; thus, the battle of good and evil raged for our souls. Satan's radar.

The presence of Satan is everywhere around us. When the potential for God's glorifying good is present, Satan is there with a hint of adrenaline rush. He's watching with a keen focus, ready to drop a small nugget of temptation in our path disguised as any number of tasty delights. Temptation is cloaked in what our human nature wants and what our spiritual nature hates. Satan is the ultimate competitor, the gladiator in the arena who thirsts for death, a spiritual death. He lurks in a red dress and high heels, he is wrapped up in a candy bar, he is waiting in a bottle of Jack Daniels, a bag of cocaine, on an internet porn site, on Facebook, he is waiting at the bottom and the top of a stack of money, he is sitting at the blackjack table, he is waiting by a bucket of fried chicken, and he loves to live in our words. Our words are powerful tools and tend to cut deeply and hurt the ones we love the most. Words created by God but used for Satan's glory. Good and evil are everywhere, always fighting, always waging for our humanity.

Once on a Wednesday afternoon, David said something that lit the light bulb over my head and stoked the fire in my heart. It was something so simple. Perhaps I had heard it before, but it sounded like fresh words. It was as if I finally heard the answer I had been seeking for a lifetime.

"What matters," he said in a nonchalant tone, "is the condition of your heart."

All of me paused.

For some odd reason, those eight words solidified all of the haphazard jigsaw pieces of my faith puzzle. I finally understood that if my heart was in tune with God, pointed toward Him at all times, then I was in harmony with my Father. That was the secret to the connection with God. Even though it didn't directly explain faith, it was all I needed to take the leap. Everything had jelled.

The most interesting part of the heart equation was that only God and I knew what the true condition of my heart really was. No one other than God can judge my commitment to Him, my heart for Him. People may think they know if their neighbor is truly a Christian; however, many things take place behind closed doors and within the heart of man that are contrary to true harmony with the Father.

With David's and Dan's guidance, I swung from the concept of Adam and Eve as fish to the probable reality of their true and factual existence. These two mentors were fishers of men. They had a profound impact on my faith journey and helped me arrive at the self-realization that I was a Christian, a label that I would have never considered before but now was a tag that I was proud to wear. The ironic part of this multiyear gathering was that we never prayed. If we did, it was only once in our comfortable upper room.

I had the answer that changed my perspective on the essential relationship with Christ. It was my heart. And from my heart all things would flow. My words and my deeds would now be a reflection of my heart, and I would be a conduit for God's love. Tall words, especially if you're on Satan's radar!

The experience leading up to salvation is as unique to each person as one's own fingerprint. For me, there was no lightning bolt or flash of light. It was a gradual growth process that bloomed over years of steady nurturing. Although my commitment to God and His saving grace grew over time, the moment that truly rooted my confirmation of faith was the August night God revealed I would spend eternity in His lap.

Tim, another successful businessman and one of my spiritual mentors, helped me understand the development of faith in the heart of man. Tim explained that our spiritual soul is like a balloon. At an early age it resembled a deflated balloon, empty, without air. But as we grew in our understanding of God, the balloon would begin to inflate.

With years of searching, questioning, and study, my balloon grew with the Holy Spirit until it was filled with the spiritual love God humbly offers to everyone; it became the essential component of my faith. Now that made sense to me. Some people may have their balloon inflated with an instant, rushing flow from a helium tank while others receive a slow, steady stream of air until it is full. The latter was me. I received a slow, steady inflation of God's spirit until He said, "Hey, Gene. There you go. Take your balloon; now fly."

Katrina

If you have come here to help me, you are wasting your time.
But if you come because your liberation is bound up with mine,
then let us work together.
—LILLA WATSON[12]

THE PEACE AND SERENITY ENGULFING me created an everlasting calm in my heart. The tumult that raged on the night of my near-death experience was a test. The spiritual warfare that battled for my yearning soul was vivid. Satan wanted me, wanted me bad. He knew I could be a powerful and persuasive force for his evil plan on earth. God, too, knew I could be a powerful and persuasive force for His ministry on earth.

God planned the night of August 31, 2005, for the keen insight of a revelation. He removed the scales from my eyes to reveal my future in his everlasting Kingdom: safe, secure, fearless. There were no worries, only joy. A part of my heart yearned for death to revel in God's glory. The other part of my heart cried for my family. So I fought and I lived so that through my leadership and new-found faith, others can live later. God blessed me that night with an unwavering confidence that heaven is real and waiting for everyone who seeks God. He gave me the rare gift of insight.

I had peace.

Six hundred miles away in New Orleans, there was no peace. There was little hope. Hell on earth reigned for the families trapped

in the cauldron of violence, murder, rape, raw sewage, and sweltering heat of the Superdome, home to the beloved New Orleans
Saints. The palpable irony of the moniker "Home of the Saints"
swung like a hangman's noose over the pit of hell for so many of
God's faithful children.

Reverend Brian was a member of a Disaster Medical Assistance
Team deployed by the government to the Superdome to ride out
the storm. They were there to comfort, heal, give hope, shine light
in the dark, and bring the ministry of heaven to hell. Brian and his
small team of medics stitched up bullet wounds, comforted people
as they died in their arms, and delivered babies while standing in
toxic raw sewage. The team treated over 800 patients before snipers
forced them to flee for their lives.

So many elderly and poor who decided to stay home because
they had no viable transportation to evacuate the city were found
months later in their attics, dead from drowning or a heart attack as
they gasped for their last precious breath while the flood waters rose
to 20 feet, well above rooflines in the humble Lower Ninth Ward.

Our brothers and sisters were dying of heat exhaustion, starva-
tion, dehydration, heart attacks, and fear. They suffered through
every second of agony that fear brings. The media swarmed New
Orleans, covering the horror of the great American city on the
bayou. But it wasn't just New Orleans; the entirety of the coastal
communities along the Gulf of Mexico had suffered various levels
of damage. Mississippi was also a primary casualty of Katrina's wrath.
For those who didn't perish during Hurricane Katrina, many more
lost everything tangible in their lives.

But America wasn't aware of the depth of the tragedy . . . just yet.

On September 1, the news reports were filling our widescreen,
high-definition TVs. Although it wasn't our direct personal problem, people, relief organizations, municipalities, and churches rallied

in an unprecedented motion of God's love. America was responding, offering food, water, clothing, money, manpower, and prayer with a yearning to reach out and help comfort the predominantly black community left behind to fend for themselves in the tumultuous wake of Katrina.

I watched the reports and I wept. My heart wept and my eyes cried for those in pain and suffering. I wanted to jump into my new midnight-blue Range Rover and drive to the Gulf to help, to lend a hand. Where I would go, what I would do, where I would stay, what I would eat were all secondary concerns to the burning in my heart to simply go. The desire to go was living in my heart but the practicality of the task outweighed the desire . . . temporarily.

On a crisp, beautiful fall Sunday, Steve stopped me in the hallway before worship. The normal conversation on Sunday with my church brothers always revolved around college football on autumn mornings. So when Steve pulled me aside, I was ready for the usual "Ohio State is a lock for the national championship," or "Man, the Tar Heels struggled yesterday!"

This Sunday was different.

"Let's go to New Orleans," Steve said with the usual tone of "Michigan doesn't have a chance this year."

"Are you serious?" I shot with a hopeful truth. "That's exactly what I've been wanting to do. I've never done anything like that before but I really feel like I need to go."

"Then let's do it," he said.

"Okay, I'm in. So are you going to organize it, put it together, or what?"

"I'll make some calls to see what we can find out and I'll check with some other guys to see if anyone else wants to go."

"That's fine, but if it's just me and you that's cool too. I'm with you. Just let me know when and where."

About a month later three vehicles packed with nine men and a load of tools trekked down I-85 to I-65 to the small fishing village of Bayou La Batre, Alabama, the film home of the Bubba Gump Shrimp Company. There was no Tom Hanks, no Bubba Gump, and no rapid response to the enormous need of this once beautiful coastal shrimping community. Many of the American fishermen had been replaced by a significant number of Vietnamese immigrants taking their shot at the American Dream.

We had no idea what was ahead for our team. The few certainties were found at the Presbyterian Church hosting us in Mobile: a place to sleep (with both snoring and non-snoring rooms, but some of these Christian men lied about their snoring prowess), breakfast and a home-cooked meal every day by the women of the church, a shower, a toilet, and a basketball court. It was a lot more luxurious than my preconceived notion of having to sleep on a cot in a tent in the middle of a muddy field.

In the aftermath of Katrina, FEMA and other organizations perfected the art of disaster response, but that would come in the subsequent years. In Katrina's swath of devastation, the process and organization of the response effort was haphazard at best. We would pick up our daily orders in an abandoned strip mall, with one of the deserted storefronts now being occupied by an overwhelmed and overworked FEMA rep or goodhearted but exhausted volunteer. Steve would pick up our stack of 3 x 5 note cards with an address and maybe a name and a word or two of what we should expect to do at that address, if we could find it.

On the way to every home, we would pass by mounds of debris, piles of good-intentioned donated clothing, downed power lines, abandoned houses, broken automobiles, and resilient neighbors holding on to a shred of hope with one hand and grasping God's promise with the other. Both hands held tightly with white knuckles, but either or both could slip at any given moment.

On those index cards, God revealed my future.

Our first touch of the utter devastation was deep in the woods down a broken and muddy road surrounded by overgrown brush. The old, beige wooden house with aqua green shutters was completely under water just a few months earlier and no one had lived in it since. Outside was a crippled, light blue, old-school Lincoln Town Car up on blocks with the doors falling off. Entering a water-damaged house months after submersion is a smell one never forgets. The mold and rotting materials in the house concocted an aroma of must and mildew that was difficult to remove from the inside of our nostrils. The stench was thick.

Our task was to gut the home to the studs and remove all furnishing and personal belongings and pile them in the ditch for waste removal. The pile grew as we dumped lumber, mattresses, tables, cabinets, clothes, insulation/asbestos and even a water-logged Bible. There was something wrong about throwing a Bible away that had been through so much, but we were told to throw away everything and never take anything away from a worksite as a souvenir.

We met the homeowner, an old black lady who looked as weathered as the Gulf coast. She was tired, hurting, disillusioned, and in need of hope. She was wearing a smile. We were there to provide hope, whether it was for all of her future or just for a day. Hope was cloaked in three vehicles carrying nine white men from South Carolina.

My heart tried to cope with the fear and agony she had been through. But she was only one—only one of hundreds of thousands just like her. So many people were in need of hope when it felt like their country and their brothers and sisters had abandoned them. We were there to help her through her long journey to a new future. She was there to help us, to help me. She couldn't have known, but on that muddy, broken road is where God called my name and said, "Gene, this is your future."

All of the work sites we assisted with that week were as diverse as the paths we all walked. The social juxtaposition was varied, but the one thing most everyone we served had in common was a low socio-economic condition. Our team was wealthy compared to those we helped. In one hour we would help descendents of slaves while the next hour found us in a house decorated with rebel flag comforters and pictures of Elvis Presley. It was not our place to evangelize or judge one's culture and racial perspectives. We were there to help rebuild and offer hope to anyone who needed it.

On our last two days in Bayou La Batre, our task appeared undoable. On an unzoned piece of land, two trailer homes rested side by side. Out back was a wooden and metal fenced dog shack with a pit-bull named Lady chained to a post. Lady had seen a lot. One trailer stood strong while Katrina's force of nature flipped the other one upside down and smashed it like an aluminum can under a boot. Fortunately no one was inside the capsized trailer during the hurricane; however, everything they owned remained inside. Our task was to remove the entire pile of what appeared to be the trailer and stack it in a ditch for the waste removers. To lighten the load, we decided to put only the metal and glass in the ditch . . . and burn the rest, with the owner's permission of course. We took axes and cut the aluminum sides of the trailer in sections then rolled the pieces, like twisting a Cuban cigar. As the ditch got fuller, the white neighbor across the street kept yelling at us from atop his John Deere tractor. It appeared that he didn't like us piling someone's home in the ditch across from his house. I wondered if he had ever offered to help before we got there.

In the early dawn hours with a heavy mist hovering over our site, we lit the fire. We burned everything—plastic, wood, insulation, furniture, wiring, everything that would burn. There was no code to adhere to; we were at a place where civilization seemed to have been forgotten. The flames licked the sky as if calling to God. The thick mist surrounded the intense fire like a burnt offering. We watched the glow and listened to the crackle. It was serene.

When the fire died down, and with the glass and metal piled high in the ditch, we rested for a moment. Looking into the eyes of the homeowners, whose great-great-grandparents had probably worked the cotton fields of the South, you could see hope. You could see a determination to fight for what was theirs, a dedication to work hard and rebuild. You could see gratefulness for a helping hand from a group of white strangers who asked for nothing in return. You could see hope.

The desire created between helping those in need and finding a place of peace within myself, to be truly useful, was unnerving. I wanted to be in New Orleans helping recover from one storm, but I also oddly wanted another hurricane or earthquake to strike without any actual loss of life. Of course I didn't actually want another disaster to happen, I simply wanted to offer hope to those in hopeless situations. By assisting in the clean-up effort of something so horrific, I felt I was providing hope. Another natural disaster meant another opportunity to help those with overwhelming desperation. I wanted to be truly useful.

: : : : : :

God was pressing me.

Back in my comfortable home, in my comfortable house, with my comfortable family, I was uncomfortable. I looked directly into my eyes in the bathroom mirror.

"What am I doing?" I asked out loud. "What in the world am I doing? I shouldn't be here fighting to build a company; I should be back down in the Gulf helping all those people rebuild their lives. I can best use my gifts helping those people find hope."

I was lost, confused, hurting. My heart was in extreme conflict with the reality of Hurricane Katrina and those left behind.

David, my theological discussion group leader, helped me through the quandary. I laid out my dilemma.

"I'm being pulled in two directions." I stated my case. "On one hand I feel I need to be doing ministry and helping the people on the Gulf rebuild. On the other hand, I've got responsibilities with the company and I can't turn my back on it."

Without hesitation he solved the problem. "Gene, you need to stay where you are. You are the CEO of the company you founded and you have obligations to your investors and clients."

Well that was that.

But God was just teasing me, preparing me for what was to come. He let me taste my future amidst a disaster in a small shrimping village in Alabama. With every disaster, something beautiful blossomed and grew. Whether it was people helping people, someone turning to Christ for the answers they sought, or people finding hope for a new beginning, devastation and disaster could result in something beautiful.

My own disaster was merely down the road. I would have to stand tall or run. I would be faced with the harsh realities of business and an economic downturn of biblical proportion. God had His hands all over me, sculpting like a potter, and He was about to put me in the kiln.

What Would Jesus Do?

"A new command I give you: Love one another.
As I have loved you, so you must love one another.
By this everyone will know that you are my disciples,
if you love one another."
—JESUS OF NAZARETH[13]

STEALING THE MONEY WAS EASY. Doing the time wasn't. Decaying in a prison cell with other convicted felons and yearning for her three young children was an unrelenting purgatory.

Prison provided barely enough air for Gwen to breathe but just enough to keep self-pity alive. She cried for her children and clutched her ragged Bible while she prayed for the pain to stop; the crying continued but the pain never ceased. The night was never kind enough to stop the empty tears.

Morning brought with it the fear of the flesh, the fear of bumping into the wrong person at the wrong time, or the panic of being caught alone in the bathroom when her protector was nowhere near. Her five-foot-four-inch malnourished frame was defenseless against the well-fed career criminals.

Morning also brought the fear of the mind. The merciless torment of the unanswerable questions, "Will my children remember me? Will my husband take me back? When will I get out of here? Will I ever get out of here? Is my attorney doing anything to help me get out of here? Where is God when I need Him most?"

Gwen's heart knew the answer to every question she asked, but her mind didn't listen.

The night brought with it dark. No words, just dark. There was always the hum of the florescent light as it leaked into the cube. The light was never any match for the dark recesses of her mind as she lay awake, eyes wide open, fearing what was behind her eyelids when exhaustion finally overwhelmed her.

Gwen's friends and family convinced themselves that she didn't belong in "there" . . . in prison. Only ruthless criminals, scum of the earth, losers, and delinquents belong behind bars. They would say she was a good person. She was a dedicated, beautiful mother and a supportive wife living in a dream house, she attended her upper/middle-class church every week in crisp new clothes, and she was happy, giving, and loving. But Gwen was also a convicted criminal, an adulterous, and a common thief.

Why?

That simple three-letter-question plagued Gwen's mind and all who knew her. It was because she was abused by her father when she was twelve. It was because she grew up in a trailer and always wanted what she didn't have. It was because she was getting back at all the guys who used her in high school and college. It was because she was leveraged to pay for all of the renovations to her country club estate. It was because she felt sorry for the contractor who was in a miserable marriage and she needed some extra money so she could properly thank him for his needed affection. It was because her victim was a very mean and vengeful man and he deserved to be punished for his own list of indiscretions and crimes.

Or was it because evil triumphed for a fleeting moment? An epic battle of temptation waged in everyone, every day. The unlawful act was an overwhelming attraction that became second nature. The allure was overwhelming when the act was first considered. Once it was considered, there was no turning back. A simple routine that was wrong, illegal, and destructive, but it felt good.

Stealing the money was easy.

: : : : : :

Gwen sat on the back row of the aluminum bleachers in the church gym. She was waiting for basketball practice to end so she could take her children to her newly renovated home on Country Club Drive. She looked distraught. Gwen's face was drawn and sad.

"What's wrong?" I asked, knowing the weight of the world with the looming trial and potential jail time was eating away at her.

"I'm just scared about the hearing," she said, even though her attorney assured her there was a very slim possibility she would ever serve any time for her crime. "I'm worried about my kids."

Her three elementary school–aged children were not aware of the wrenching situation at hand and had no idea their loving mother could be taken away in a police bus and sent ninety miles away to a state prison in Columbia.

Gwen had gotten caught embezzling money from her employer, the same crime many women who were in her similar job position had been convicted of. Her open access to bank accounts from a trusting boss put her in a place of extreme responsibility, a place of trust where temptation and the constant battle between good and evil raged. Gwen's temptation wasn't food or pornography or alcohol or drugs or gambling. It was the easy access to cash and the self-denial that no one would ever find out if she lifted a few dollars. Weakness and temptation live within everyone, and when the door is open to giving in to that temptation, Satan boots the door wide open.

Even though she had stolen around $20,000, her employer swore she had embezzled over $300,000 from his business and personal accounts. What made matters worse was the vengeful nature of her superior, the business owner. He didn't want to forgive and forget with restitution of the $20,000; he wanted repayment of the alleged $300,000 plus a maximum prison sentence of 40 years. He was not turning the other cheek; he was trying to bury Gwen alive.

Adding additional misery, Gwen had given in to the temptation of sexual sin, a sin that has the power to emerge within anyone if the circumstances align into the perfect storm. While stealing the money, she was having an affair with another man who was showing her loving affection. Her storm was at hurricane force. When some of her closest friends found out about her transgressions, they cut her off from support and rapidly evacuated. Gwen was slowly being left alone to deal with her sin and legal battle by herself, alone and sinking fast. Gwen was stranded, burdened with her sin, and fearful of the ramifications of her crime.

My wife, Mary, was friendly with Gwen, as she was with most everyone in the church. She was not a close personal friend but simply a friend. Gwen turned to Mary with her saga and Mary listened. She became a close friend to the woman and was the recipient of Gwen's life story: the good, the bad, and the ugly. Mary and a couple of other women were there for Gwen when so many others disassociated from her, casting her aside because of her errors. Mary set a God-like example of helping and loving someone in need, at the risk of being associated with a known criminal and adulteress.

Gwen was every person, trying to improve her life from her frightful childhood while fighting temptation. She struggled to break the bonds that were dragging her down. She met her husband as a senior in high school, a young man with aspirations of accomplishing great things. Growing up in a poor environment in Alabama, she broke the vicious cycle and attended a major university. Gwen graduated and was living the American dream in an affluent subdivision with three kids, a dog, and a minivan. From the outside, she seemingly had it all. But real truth dwells within the walls of one's home but more importantly within one's heart, where the real battles are desperately fought.

Sitting in the church gym, Gwen was living in the tortured state of not knowing what the future held. "Would the lawsuit settle? Would it go to trial? What about my kids? What about my marriage? Will I go to jail? Oh my God, what if I go to jail?" she tormented herself daily.

I saw a young lady, one in my community of siblings, a fellow church member, hurting. I was part of the body of the church and we were called to help and love our brothers and sisters under all circumstances. The mission trip to Bayou La Batre was still on fire in my heart with a strong desire to help others, and now here was a perfect opportunity to help one of our own. I wanted to help, but what could *I* do?

Gwen was now an open book. I began questioning her about the potential legal ramifications, nuances her lawyer suggested that could help lessen the charges or sentence, and anything else that I could glean to find my place for a corner of support. I did not judge her for her faults nor did I condone any of her behavior. It was not my place. My place was to assist my sister as Jesus would have assisted me.

At no time did Gwen ever ask me to help her.

She mentioned that the judge would probably look favorably upon her during the hearings if she could offer restitution and pay back the amount she claims she stole, $20,000. Gwen was broke and had limited resources. Her husband, a notable attorney, was still reeling from the wealth of information he was being drowned with. Her family in Alabama was in no position to help, as they were trying to simply meet their monthly bills. Gwen was at a dead end. My question to myself was simple and direct: "What would Jesus do?"

That was it, I thought. *This is my opportunity to help.*

Although my financial capacity was limited, I knew I could donate something to chip away at the $20,000 goal. I had been successful with rallying support, financial and otherwise, with other causes, so I should easily be able to collect $20,000 of financial support for a church member in need.

Gwen was humbled by my offer to help raise some money in support of her case and she was overwhelmingly thankful. I simply figured that if I were in her position, I would hope there would be someone out there willing to help me in the same way, someone to pick up my flag and carry it when I became too weak. I would hope there were people out there that truly embodied the golden rule regardless of the consequences. I would hope someone would love me as Jesus loved them.

Even though I felt confident I could help her get close to raising the twenty grand, this was different. Gwen had broken both God's laws and man's law. Who knew how people would react? *How would the people in our church respond?* I thought.

: : : : : :

Mary was supportive of my offer to help Gwen. She said it sounded ambitious, but she was behind me and would also help in any way she could.

The first calls were to my closest church friends. I outlined the situation that Gwen was faced with. Some gave without hesitation; others wanted more information. While visiting my parent's house in Florida, my mother overheard one of my phone calls asking for money with a detailed explanation of the issue. Before my call was complete, Mom had written an unsolicited check for $100 to help someone she had never met. She was compelled to help someone in trouble. With every call came the challenge of asking for something good in support of something bad. Although Gwen was remorseful, regretful, and saddened by her deeds, her prior actions were bad; but her relationship with Christ was growing.

Raising the first $5,000 was relatively easy. Then support began to wane. As my dedication to making calls slowed, so did the support. My commitment to helping Gwen needed to be stepped up; the donations to her cause reflected directly how hard I fought for her. I got more aggressive with the phone calls and the personal requests.

People at church who I really didn't know came up to me and handed me checks with a simple "Thank you for what you are doing." A close friend who was out of work and struggling to make ends meet even gave me a check; although I tried to refuse the gift, he insisted.

Of the approximately thirty people I asked, only two told me no and another three gave no reply after my appeal and a follow up. Those who declined or offered no reply grieved me. I had to fight my internal resentment of those who did not help Gwen.

"These are our church members, my friends," I told Mary. "If we can't count on them, who can we count on?"

I became angry within my heart toward my affluent friends who I knew had the discretionary funds to help but turned their back on the situation; even a $10 donation was a gesture of good faith in helping our struggling sister. I had to fight my own angst and remember when I asked for support that it was not a command but a request. My confidence was altered as I expected every appeal to return a pledge of support. It was as though this campaign was an exercise God was putting me through to help humble me and teach me that not everyone is on the same quest. It was a daily struggle to keep my personal anger in check against a few of my friends.

This was not about Gwen, and this was not about me. This was about what God would have us do in times of trial and how we should be obedient to Him and trust in His love. It was about what Jesus would have done if faced with the same circumstances.

:::::::

Jason called me over to a table in the fellowship hall after a church meeting. He was well dressed, as usual, and suave with his well-groomed, sandy-blonde hair.

"Gene, can I ask you something?" he said.

"Sure, anything."

"I really admire the things you do with the mission trips and helping others; how do you do it?" This was one of the church's deacons asking a simple lay person how to serve.

"Do what?"

"Well, I'd like to do more but I'm really not sure what else I should do. Mission trips might not be my thing, but I'd like to continue to do more in the community."

"Just find some things that move your heart and mean something to you and simply do it. Ask questions and follow through on whatever service passion you have."

During the conversation my heart started beating a little faster. I knew Jason's wife had pulled her friendship from Gwen as she found out the details of her sins. She had become very vocal to other church members and clergy about where the church should stand regarding Gwen's precarious situation. Since Jason and his wife were now estranged from Gwen, I hadn't asked them about helping her cause. But now I couldn't help myself. "Knowing what I know about Gwen and your wife, I have a way you could really show God's love," I confidently said.

"What's that?"

"I'm not asking, but I would say as a family you could show God's love by making a donation to help Gwen's restitution."

There was an awkward silence.

I waited with eager anticipation for a reply. I let the pause hang for a moment. "But I want you to know," as I rescued him, "I'm not asking. I do want you to consider it though."

Jason had something to think about, but it certainly wasn't what he was expecting when he first called me over.

That went well, I thought.

I felt it was becoming my place to start pressing people to at least think about their walk. I was certainly no model of Christianity, but I was trying to walk in the steps of Jesus. I was trying to use His words in my conversation with others. I was trying.

: : : : : :

The donations began to pick up but not nearly enough to reach $20,000 by the hearing date. I pressed harder.

I gave a lot of consideration to the conversation with Jason. I heard more secondhand information about how his wife disapproved of my support of Gwen and how she was vocally opposed to my actions. It irritated me.

I called Jason.

"Hey man, remember what we talked about the other day regarding Gwen and how I wasn't asking you to help her?" I began.

"Yes," he said.

"Well, now I'm asking," I said with reserved aggression. "I'd like for you and your wife to contribute to Gwen's cause."

"Wow, okay. I have to talk to my wife about it, but I'll let you know."

"Thanks. And keep in mind I'm not asking for any specific amount; it could be $5. It's whatever you feel you can do."

It didn't take long before I got a call from the missus.

: : : : : :

The body of the church was responding, but it was time to see where the church itself stood. I felt the issue needed to be pressed as hard and as far as possible. I asked both the senior pastor and the associate pastor to contribute. They did without hesitation.

There was one final request that needed to take place—the Board of Deacons, the church itself. I knew it was an issue that could potentially turn church brothers and sisters against each other, but I was prepared for the fallout. It was an unprecedented bombshell I was dropping within the walls of my church, but it needed to be launched. The Church *is* God's love.

With brazen resolve I asked the senior pastor, "Allen, what do I have to do to ask the church to support Gwen's cause?"

"Just ask," he calmly replied.

"Okay, I'm formally asking."

"I'll bring it up to the diaconate and I'll let you know after our next meeting."

"Great."

Jason was a deacon and a vocal part of the lively discussion. With a rare split vote, the diaconate approved the financial request to support Gwen by a slim margin. The church stepped up and bravely did the very thing Jesus would have done. It made me proud to be a member of our congregation.

Soon after the deacons' difficult decision, Jason and his family left the church.

With the court hearing fast approaching, the financial support was nearly half of the $20,000 I aggressively sought. Although I felt my efforts failed her, it was nevertheless a significant sum gathered from a small group of caring people.

: : : : : :

On an unusually chilly but sunny April afternoon, Gwen's highly publicized court hearing took place. The newspaper and local television stations were lying in wait of the verdict. There were a couple dozen church members, family, and friends in attendance to show physical and monetary support for our sister in peril.

In the case before Gwen's, a deacon from another church had been caught molesting and having sexual relations with an under-age member of his congregation. The judge gave him a slap on the wrist and probation for his offenses.

I thought that was a good sign—a soft-hearted judge.

Gwen handed her purse to my wife. "Here, hold this for me until after the hearing," she said. Gwen knew she would be right back with probation and community service.

She pled guilty on the advice of her counsel and the hope of leniency based on partial restitution and a plan for full repayment. With the victim of her crime adamantly pressing the maximum sentence of forty years in prison, the hearing was tense and the courtroom was filled with palpable anxiety.

Gwen stood before the judge next to an oversized bailiff.

The judge spoke. Her sentence—ten years in prison, suspended to seven with three year's probation. Her sentence was to begin immediately.

Gwen turned around and looked with utter disbelief over what the judge said. Her knees went weak as the bailiff grabbed her arm. Her eyes closed and she fell to the floor in momentary blackness.

She was ushered out the side of the dazed courtroom as the door slammed behind her. The people in the courtroom were shocked.

Gwen served nineteen months total behind bars, away from her friends, away from her church, away from her children. She was alone.

: : : : : :

Through the entire ordeal, there was overwhelming support and thanks offered to Mary and me from our church friends for our commitment to raise money for our sister in trouble. It was truly humbling. One church member stopped my wife one afternoon.

"Mary, I just want to say thank you," he said. "I'm a very black and white person. That's how I see things. I want to thank you because you and Gene helped me see that there is gray."

I felt I did the right thing. I felt I showed unconditional love as we have been taught to do. I felt I did what Jesus would have done; however, I was uncertain about the feelings of those elders, deacons, and church members who did not approve of my actions. I was uncertain about my place at my church.

The Church Machine

His voice leads us not into timid discipleship but into bold witness.
—CHARLES STANLEY[14]

WITH NEW-FOUND ENTHUSIASM FOR MISSIONS and helping our fellow man, I became a vocal church member for helping
those less fortunate and in distress. I wanted to be where there was
pain and suffering so I might offer a ray of hope. I wanted to be a
simple conduit of God's love and His shining light. God worked me
over on the muddy back roads of Alabama in the wake of a horren-
dous tragedy. I aggressively urged other church members, clergy, and
our deacons to consider disaster relief projects through Presbyterian
Disaster Assistance as a means to fulfilling our church's calling.

God massaged my heart to help a struggling church member in
need. I was on a mission to walk in Jesus' footprints at whatever
cost. My style was unfiltered and aggressive. It wasn't everyone's
cup of tea. A former employee once told me, "Gene, people either
love you or hate you; there's no in-between." It didn't matter. I
knew the risk of calling people out to face a hard decision and
answer a question they would rather avoid.

The fire in my soul was lit, and anyone who cared to glance in my
direction saw the flame burning. The blaze didn't go unnoticed.

When Derrick approached me at Wednesday night supper, I
thought I was in for the usual Duke versus North Carolina banter.
He was his normal church self: superb posture, neatly cropped

haircut, conservative three-button suit with a white oxford shirt and a tightly knotted vertical-striped tie from an exclusive men's clothier. He wore his usual lawyerly smirk with unusual anticipation. Derrick was ready to pop the question.

We walked near a wall inside the lobby of the church to gain a moment of peace from the Crayola-covered children's table in the fellowship hall. High-pitched laughter swirled around the kiddie table that was swarmed by a dozen of our precious youth.

Derrick had a question. He peered with stoic confidence. He was primed to ask me the question (or was it a statement?) as if my answer determined life or death.

"Gene," Derrick said in his to-the-point monotone calm. "You've been nominated by one of your peers and the session would like for you to sit on the diaconate and serve as a deacon of the church."

"What?!" I blurted with absolute astonishment.

"We would like for you to accept the invitation to become a member of the diaconate," he confirmed.

"I don't think so. Becoming a part of the church bureaucracy is something I swore I would never do. I don't want to be a part of all that."

"I think it's something you need to do," Derrick confidently rebutted as if he could win me over to the dark side with his Blue Devil persuasion.

"Derrick, I don't know what to say," I offered as I tried to remove myself from the question, but it was too late. He had me trapped in a Coach K full-court press. "I'm extremely honored that I would be considered, but if you want an answer right now, the answer would have to be no. I just don't think it's for me."

I paused. He stared.

Silence.

"I'll tell you what I'll do; I'll think about it," I eased.

"Take all the time you need."

We shook hands with the usual "Tar Heel versus Blue Devil, my death-grip handshake is more solid than yours" finale.

I escaped. I broke the press! I can deal with this later. But I knew it wasn't over. I knew it was something I had to face. I knew I would need to talk to Mary about it, I knew I would need to ask my minister about it, and I knew I would need to ask God about it. The problem was I knew what the answer was before I asked the question. I may have been out of Derrick's grip, but I knew I was still trapped.

We walked back into the fellowship hall, past the clamor of the children's table, cutting through the announcements over the loud speaker and the cacophony of voices enjoying the fried chicken and macaroni and cheese. I heard nothing. I was in a silent movie trying to speak.

Days passed. Weeks passed and I couldn't get if off my mind. *Why would they want me representing my church as a deacon? I really don't know that much about the Bible and I really still feel lost at times,* I kept thinking to myself. *I ruffled a lot of well-groomed feathers with the whole Gwen issue, so why would I even be considered? I know nothing about being a deacon except that they have a lot of laborious meetings.* Being a deacon was nowhere on my bucket list.

I was so far from a keen understanding of what the Presbyterian Church actually stood for. I didn't know what "we" as Presbyterians believed. They talked of doctrine. What's a doctrine? I heard talk of John Calvin in the Bible and Theology class, but I wasn't really sure who he was. He sounded like an apostle at times, but I knew he wasn't mentioned in the Bible. Even the weekly corporate prayer of confession, which many churches used, set me on edge. I simply didn't agree with what we recited in unison on any given Sunday. A typical corporate prayer of confession usually sounded something like this:

Holy, holy, holy God of grace, love and communion, we confess that we have failed to love you with all our heart, soul, and, mind; and to love our neighbor as ourselves. We ignore your commandments, stray from your way, and follow other gods. Have mercy on us. Forgive our sin and raise us to new life that we may serve you faithfully and give honor to your holy name. Amen.[15]

My lack of true understanding fooled me into believing that I never failed to love God, that I never strayed from His commandments, and that I certainly didn't follow other gods. I felt I had to recite something that was contrary to the truth, Presbyterian or not.

Furthermore, I had no idea what Presbyterians were as opposed to other denominations—we all worshiped Jesus. I simply liked the people in our church, the adult and youth programs, and the solemn nature of the worship service. My knowledge bank was empty of what a Presbyterian truly was. I was a Catholic (well, once a Catholic, always a Catholic) and now I'm wearing the cloak of a protestant. I didn't have the same faith that the other people in my church did. They seemed to be so in-touch with God and Jesus and Paul and all the stories in the Bible. Why did they want me to serve the church in an official role?

A couple of weeks passed and I set an appointment with Allen, the well-respected, revered theologian and minister at our church. We sat at the weathered four-top table in his office at the foot of a mountainous wall of books. Allen was renowned for his knowledge and analytic approach to delivering the Word of God. His sermons were very deliberate, very calculated, and extremely cerebral. He was a theologian's theologian.

I often sat in church on Sunday and listened to his sermons, thinking it sounded like he was delivering the Word in the original Greek or Hebrew. His theology was so advanced I had a hard time listening, much less comprehending the message. To me, his sermons were often dull and lifeless with an occasional moment of *wow*. I later realized the problem was the receiver, not the deliverer. I was not listening, I was not hearing. Once I opened my ears and heart, his sermons were bright and vibrant, full of useful information that later enriched my heart and understanding of the Scripture. I liked Allen and respected him; I just didn't understand him, until I listened.

Since he was the leader of our congregation, I felt it was my obligation to take Derrick's request seriously and see if I could remove myself from the process by asking Allen to withdraw my candidacy.

After a sip of Maxwell House from the ceramic mug, I stated my peace.

"Allen, you don't want someone like me as a deacon in this church," I proclaimed. "You know I am fairly unfiltered and I am liable to say things I shouldn't."

"On the contrary, Gene," he said with his serious smile, "you're exactly who we want."

"What do you mean?"

"You are exactly what the diaconate needs."

I interrupted. "But Allen, I'm a different kind of person. I'm not going to go along with a vote for the sake of the vote. I can be a wrecking ball. You remember what happened when I stepped up to seek support for Gwen—it made a lot of people mad. In any given situation I will frankly speak my mind. There's a chance I'll get some people ticked off. Are you really sure?"

"Gene, you were the only candidate that was unanimous."

We sat in silence.

We spoke a bit more; I tried to give him a laundry list of reasons why I wasn't the guy for the job:

I don't want to be a part of the church machine.

I'm pretty busy and I'm not sure if my schedule will permit it.

I would just rather be a member of the congregation.

I really don't know anything about the Presbyterian Church.

I don't think I'm adequately equipped to be a deacon.

What if I embarrass the church?

Aren't there better-qualified candidates?

Blah, blah, blah, blah, blah!

After some more pondering, deflection, and offered excuses why I would be a horrible deacon, I left. I was losing the battle.

I could feel the question wearing me down. But I wanted no part of the righteous administration of any church. I just wanted to teach children's Sunday school from time to time, attend church events, hang out with my friends, help others as my heart leads, eat at Wednesday night supper, go to service on Sunday, and watch my kids grow up in the church. I wasn't trying to be a leader in the church machine.

Being a deacon wouldn't help me get into heaven. I had felt the hand of God in August, and I knew I would spend eternity with Him. The church machine was not in my plan . . . I didn't want to be a deacon in any church.

Mary and I spoke about this regularly. She could see the stress that the consideration caused me. What kept creeping into my head were the intolerable challenges Mary had faced when she served on the diaconate. She was assigned to the personnel committee when there were some drastic personnel changes being made in the church. There were laboriously long phone calls, emotional meetings, and many tears. There were times when our family was an afterthought to the priority of her duty as a deacon, or so it seemed.

I didn't want any of that additional stress and time commitment. My life was filled with enough stress without the church machine dragging me down and out of sight of me.

We talked and prayed.

I resisted.

We talked.

I resisted.

I agreed, "I'll do it."

I finally called Derrick and broke the news: "Okay," giving in to the force pulling me to a place I was destined to be, "I'll do it."

"Thank you, Gene. We appreciate it."

"My pleasure. I'm happy and honored to serve. Just let me know what I need to do. I pray I don't let you down."

And that was that. I was now a part of the machine, the man-made church machine. I did what I said I wouldn't do. But I knew—we all knew—it's what I needed. Quite simply, I had no say in the matter. The decision wasn't mine.

It was God's.

It was an honor to just be considered, and serving on the dia-conate was an enormous responsibility to fulfill. I would take it extremely seriously. I had been a follower who looked up to the leadership, and now I was a part of the leadership with a congrega-tion looking to me and the other deacons and elders for guidance. The accountability and trust placed in me and the other candidates was not to be taken with a light heart or passive dedication. It was time to formally serve the body of Christ and continue to ask a simple question with every decision facing us, just as I did with Gwen: "What would Jesus do?"

Caroline Bear and a Million Prayers

To everyone who's lost someone they love
Long before it was their time
You feel like the days you had were not enough
when you said goodbye

There is hope for the helpless
Rest for the weary
Love for the broken heart
There is grace and forgiveness
Mercy and healing
He'll meet you wherever you are
Cry out to Jesus, Cry Out to Jesus.
—THIRD DAY[16]

IT'S EASY TO MAKE A tangible difference and show God's love in a disaster area: rebuild a house. It's easy to make a tangible difference and show God's love when a friend is in a financial crisis: give a gift of money and help raise additional support. It's a different story when a friend is struck down with a potentially terminal illness. Our tangible difference turns into an intangible plea. It's a terrible, helpless feeling when you want to help save a life but can do nothing about it . . . except pray.

: : : : : :

The candle flickered in the middle of the large atrium–like room. The ceiling capped our presence as all 250 eyes were fixed on the light. The burning flame seemed to be a sign of hope for the 125 people pleading for a miracle. About 50 people, mostly women and children, sat on the chairs arranged in a neat circle on the white tile floor. Another 75 of us, mainly men and women, stood in a circle behind the group of chairs. Everyone was holding hands. It was like a scene out of Avatar, the inhabitants of Pandora, pleading and chanting for life in a circle around the Tree of Souls.

My palms were clammy. But what did it matter? I was holding the hands of two men on each side of me, one I knew and the other I did not. My right hand seemed to be sweatier than the left, and of course that was the one holding the stranger's hand. But what did it matter?

We were surrounded by birth and death, tears of joy and tears of suffering, a place of hope and a place of hopelessness. Hospitals are reminders of our infinite helplessness, a place where things are out of our control. We turn our faith over to the human hands of doctors and nurses while shouting out to God our petition for help and healing. Hospitals are the common ground where life meets death and death meets eternal life. Hope is a blessed gift, if you can find it hidden in the sorrow.

Hospitals are like churches. God is called upon in every moment:

"Thank You, God."

"Damn You, God!"

"Thank You, God, for our healthy baby."

"Please, God, give her one more day."

"God, please help my mother through her surgery."

"God, how could You let this happen?"

"Please, God, give my brother strength as he is struggling with this horrible disease."

"Thank You, God."

"I pray that You steady the hand of the surgeon."

"Thank You for the loving care of the nurses."

"God, if You help him I will never sin again."

"There is no God!"

"Praise be to God!"

"Thank You, God."

"Where are You, God?"

"God, please cure my son, Jack, of cancer . . ."

During a class reunion, one accomplished and renowned doctor let me know his thoughts on God. "I don't believe in God anymore," he matter-of-factly said. "I used to, but after everything I have seen children go through, I don't believe in a God. There can't be a God."

"Then what do you think happens after one dies?" I pushed, because I knew he was well acquainted with the daily ritual of life and death.

"Nothing. I think there is nothing."

"I don't believe that," I continued. "I have faith there is a heaven that awaits us all, a place where we will be made new and become one with God."

The flame danced across the top of the candle as if it were being serenaded by a Brahms lullaby. It burned bright as if beckoning the sky above, to implore God's grace, to evoke life from the oxygen through which it thrived.

We were all there to pray for Jack. Little Jack. He was lying in his hospital bed just a few floors above, clutching the stuffed animal he named Caroline Bear next to his parents, the soft and safe teddy bear my daughter, Caroline, gave him months before. Caroline had spent countless hours babysitting Jack before and after cancer attacked his body. She was close to him; she loved him like a little brother. We were there to pray for a bright and beautiful three-year-old boy stricken with cancer. Seeing a child suffer will cause most anyone to question their faith and the existence of God, but not the faith of Molly Beth and Harold, Jack's parents. It appeared, at least to the majority of their friends and family, that their faith in God was unwavering. The ones that had the right to question the most were most firmly grounded with God's plan.

Jack's story is not unique; unfortunately it is told every day somewhere in this tortured world. His life-and-death struggle was something a little boy or girl should never have to endure, at least in our plan.

Molly Beth was washing Jack's playful body as she did every night. Warm water, bubbles, and laughter filled the tub. While rubbing her hand across his tummy, she noticed a bulge under his skin.

He was admitted to the hospital the next day and was diagnosed with Stage 4 Neuroblastoma within a week. The viciously aggressive tumor was located in his abdomen, and the cancer was also found in his lymph nodes, pancreas, and bone marrow. Jack was in trouble. He was in the fight for his life.

A sample of Molly Beth's journal posts on the CaringBridge website best tell her and her family's journey of prayer and faith down a long and frightening road.[17]

MONDAY, DECEMBER 03, 2007 06:39 PM, CST
[Eight days after Molly Beth felt the bump on Jack's belly]
This morning Jack had an MRI and did really well with that. He rested well this afternoon. Now it is nearly 7pm and we should begin the chemo shortly which will take

about an hour. He will have the same treatment daily through Friday. Please pray for minimal discomfort for him and for the medicine to be as effective as possible. Thank you for checking on us!

MONDAY, DECEMBER 03, 2007 09:08 PM, CST
The chemo plan is "one week on, three weeks off" for approximately 6 months. Although this has been a long week, today is a turning point. The chemo will help shrink the tumor and kill off the rest of the invading cancer. Once the chemo is complete, the goal is to surgically remove the tumor.

MONDAY, DECEMBER 10, 2007 07:43 AM, CST
We are home! How wonderful to all be together again—and for Jack to be in his own bed. He has an appointment tomorrow morning in the clinic. He will most likely receive blood and a medication, as well as having his counts tested. We feel that the biggest challenge right now is getting him to eat. He does not want anything it seems, and he has lost a lot of weight over the two week period. We also have to keep him from germs as much as possible since his ability to fight infection is compromised. This is so hard since he wants to see his friends. Thanks for checking on us, and for your continued prayers.

The anguished journey was well underway for the Huffman family. Jack returned to the hospital with a fever and a surgically implanted stint in his chest. His light blonde hair began to fall out, matching the countless tears his parents shed in private. Molly Beth and Harold were also dealing with the overall wellbeing of Jack's big sister, Elizabeth, as they began to take wonder in the many things formerly taken for granted.

THURSDAY, DECEMBER 20, 2007 11:55 AM, CST
Jack tolerated the chemo well yesterday. He even ate a whole grilled cheese sandwich after! Funny how we get so excited about these things now! He was not quite as happy earlier in the day. . . . When he realized we were going to the clinic (this involves a finger prick) then heading back to the hospital, he began to cry. A few of his comments were, "I don't want to go back there . . . this is where they do the hurt things . . . are we not spending the night?" We talked, had a prayer, and he was a little better. Then more crying when we entered the building, followed by screams and fighting during the blood work. I must say that I believe this strong will of Jack's is exactly what is needed to get through this.
Overall I think Jack and Elizabeth, his sister, (who by the way had two teeth extracted this AM) are both handling all of this rather well. E is trying so hard, we can tell. Jack is a little more himself lately—he does not like the staff to tease or distract him during any of the work, just do it and move on . . . then is happy to play with his family members who are around, or watch videos. He has commented that he does not have much hair anymore (like Grandad)! E misses him and prays every night that God will make him well . . . we all do, and know that you do too. Thank you.

As each day pressed forward with the fearful question mark of the unknown, Molly Beth placed her trust and faith in God that her son would be healed. She knew the devilish cancer would not relent, nor would her thanksgiving to Jack's Creator.

FRIDAY, FEBRUARY 01, 2008 04:06 PM, CST
The scan was fine! We are home and Jack feels GREAT. The last two nights we all rested a little better. This week was a little more challenging than those of late. I had a dear friend remind me today to be still, listen, know that He is God. Another thing . . . our sermon last week included, and two friends (who would not have known) sent me this . . . "Be strong and courageous. Do not be afraid or discouraged" (1 Chronicles 22:13). When we focus on our fears we forget God's faithfulness.
I would like to ask you all to please pray for Harold, myself, and Jack's doctors as we continue to make important decisions regarding his health. Our family feels the power of your prayers and the warmth of your love and friendship. What a beautiful blessing. We are so very thankful. Hug everyone a little tighter and have a great weekend!

As the family of a cancer patient, the Huffmans' world intersected with countless other families whose children also suffered from Neuroblastoma. Molly Beth could always see through the pain of the affliction. She wrote, "This world of Neuroblastoma is not a pretty one, but the beauty that God brings out of it is miraculous."

The calendar marked days, weeks, and months, and many precious children they had the privilege of getting to know were lost to the infernal cancer. When children exited this life and entered the kingdom of heaven, the reality of life would sit heavier in the back of the Huffmans' minds, reminding them of the unspoken possibility.

Jack's reports would ride a roller coaster of results to match the ride of emotions. One day the tumor decreased; the next it appeared to gain in size. One day he would be slow and listless, the next, dancing to the Backyardigans.

All hope pointed to imminent surgeries and the waiting result of the doctors' efforts.

THURSDAY, MARCH 13, 2008 04:05 PM, CST

Jack is resting peacefully. The surgery was a long one. The abdominal tumor and the lung nodule were removed. A pseudo cyst was found and taken care of properly. Jack handled the seven hours well and had a fabulous team. Some of them may know what we are certain of . . . God is controlling this for us. We are learning to listen and follow as never before. I have had to pray hard for any fear or doubt to be taken away so that He could take control. Do you think He was testing my peace about this when Jack's doctor returned to work this week (from vacation) with his arm in a sling?! Oh yes, he did. (I had to share this for a little comic relief.)

WEDNESDAY, MARCH 26, 2008 09:18 AM, CST

. . . He will be admitted Monday for the sixth chemotherapy. We appreciate prayers for no negative side effects from the medicine. Our hearts tell us he is healed, and his body is continuing to show signs of this. Jack said to me yesterday, "There is just a little bit left." I am so thankful that our Healer has given us the specific people and medicine that have treated Jack's cancer and helped our family. Please remember a precious little girl named Kris when you pray. She is having difficulty with a relapse of Neuroblastoma.

FRIDAY, APRIL 11, 2008 03:20 PM, CST

. . . Our prayers continue to be filled with praise for the healing God has provided for Jack already. We trust that He will continue providing exactly what Jack needs to be completely healthy. We appreciate all of your prayers for the same, his medical team, and our sweet Elizabeth. She loves her brother very much . . . some days are just a little harder.

On more than one occasion Harold has mentioned he wishes he could take the cancer out of Jack and put it in his own body. It dawned on me that this is something that Jesus has already done . . . "By His stripes we are healed." We fully expect that Jack's healing will be on this side of heaven.

Molly Beth and Harold were still stuck on the emotional roller coaster of treatments and surgeries, love and hope, certainty and uncertainty. The roller coaster operator pushed the lever to maximum and then left the park . . . with Molly Beth and Harold in the back seat watching Jack ride alone in the front seat.

Our community of family and friends tried to be comforting at some level, but our own ineptness to fathom their emotional state was clear. My daughters, Caroline and Alexis, understood the potential result of Jack's cancer but never wanted to talk about it. They just wanted to hold him and love him, praying that he would be healed.

"How do we comfort? How do we care? How do we relate to someone who is at risk of losing their child?" we all asked. Only those who have gone through it and lost a child could truly empathize. Their greatest refuge, undoubtedly, was God, for He also lost a Child to this world.

SATURDAY, APRIL 19, 2008 10:56 AM, CST
Jack's MIBG results confirmed the MRI . . . there is an
area of cancer still in the abdomen. The doctor will remove it Wednesday. This was not what we expected from
the results—although Jack did say to us before, "there is a
little bit left" didn't he? The peace that God continues to
provide is just one of the many blessings we are receiving,
as we continue daily to leave this in His hands. Just yesterday I read some thoughts from a friend of ours. His focus
was on the freedom and rest that come from a walk with
God . . . rather than the rules and deeds that are more often
associated with Christian faith. I could not agree more at
this moment. We would certainly be thankful for prayers
Wednesday especially, as Jack endures another surgery.

Molly Beth wrote, "My prayer is for Jack to be healed to total
heath, and I have given that to God. Thank you for praying for Him
to reign during this . . . and for strength for Jack and the rest of us."
Her CaringBridge posts increasingly revealed her dependence and
complete surrender to God. She continued, "Thank goodness when
I listen to my heart I can hear 'I am with you.' My son can too."

MONDAY, MAY 12, 2008 01:53 PM, CST
I have had several people ask me how I am so strong. It is
God . . . and this is part of how He is blessing us. Thank
you all for the precious messages, gifts, meals, transportation, and prayers. I have had many happy tears lately over
your heartfelt kindness.

SATURDAY, MAY 17, 2008 07:17 PM, CST
. . . These drugs have lists from which I have to turn away.

I keep telling myself we were given this protocol for his healing, and we have not been guided away. God has reminded me about the men walking through the fiery furnace (Daniel 3:27). The fire had not harmed their bodies, nor was a hair of their heads singed; their robes were not scorched, and there was no smell of fire on them. With my believing heart I see Jack growing into a healthy man, free from any harm of the cancer God is fighting with and for him as a four year old little boy.

SUNDAY, JUNE 08, 2008 01:42 PM, CST

. . . I turned to my trusty *Streams in the Desert* devotional a few minutes ago, and wouldn't you know I opened it to the page which included Isaiah 24:15. A couple of sentences that stood out to me were these: ". . . We are to believe that out of this is coming something more for His praise than could have come but for this fiery trial. We can only go through some fires with a large faith; little faith will fail. We must have the victory *in* the furnace." It also included Col. 2:15, "Triumphing over them *in* it" saying, "That is the real triumph—triumphing over sickness, *in* it; triumphing over death, *dying*; triumphing over adverse circumstances, *in* them." I so needed to read this today, as I had a pang of sadness watching a little boy (about Jack's age) eating breakfast with his mom at the hotel this morning. I reminded myself that Jack is triumphing over this sickness, *in* it . . . now.

THURSDAY, JUNE 12, 2008 05:04 PM, CST

Friends, the last six to seven months have been the darkest in our family. It has been this same time that we have truly relinquished control to God, thus allowing ourselves to experience His grace as never before. Here is a bit we are seeing today . . . Jack's counts are so high that his team is discontinuing the medicine that helps this process—he does not need it! Also, he is being discharged from the hospital tomorrow, 11 days after transplant!

SUNDAY, JULY 20, 2008 03:54 PM, CST

I have a book of devotionals which was given to me by a dear friend and neighbor. What I love about this book is that Sarah would find time to be alone and quiet. During this special time, she would write what she felt God was communicating to her. I find these devotionals so powerful. Here are some words from the last two days . . . "Glorifying and enjoying Me is a higher priority than maintaining a tidy, structured life. Give up your striving to keep everything under control—an impossible task and a waste of precious energy." HELLO!! She goes on to write that God's guidance for each of us is unique. Through reading her book in recent months, I have discovered that I really need to focus on tuning out the "static" of our daily lives. It really is so noisy and busy. Haven't you too noticed we are all trying to simplify anyway? Always searching for the 5 in 1 gadget, quick meal, and latest organization plan? Enough! I have found that if I will cut off the radio, screens, whatever, for a moment—perhaps when I'm feeling a little anxious—I can say, "Jesus, thank you for this husband who is working so hard, and is such a precious father. Thank you for these children who are healthy enough at the moment to bicker as siblings do. Thank you for this house—even with the shingles falling off of the roof. Please direct our steps today. Please let us hear your voice, or see you in the faces of our family or dear friends. Even perhaps, in the nurse or doctor we see today. Please sharpen our senses to notice these subtle ways in which you communicate with us. Thank you for doing it." We have to seek Him above all else in order to find Him. Often, I see Him in those of you who are reading this entry.

Normal is elusive. Every person's normal is different, or perhaps it is just reality. For the Huffmans, their normal had been forgotten, but it would creep back into their life and offer joy in what would have been a "normal" stress.

WEDNESDAY, SEPTEMBER 10, 2008 04:35 PM, CST
... He went to school for an hour and a half before his appointments. He changed his mind about being there once we arrived, then stayed. When I returned to pick him up, I could hardly get him to leave! As I recall, this is normal behavior for his age ... perhaps a little exaggerated by our situation. How nice to have "normal" things to occur. I had to remind myself of this as I was pushing Elizabeth out of the door for school as well! (I am telling you it seemed I had run a marathon before 10am rolled around.) Today, however, was smooth for both of them. We are finding our "routine for now" and are just so thankful that it involves all of us, at home together. What a blessing.

THURSDAY, SEPTEMBER 18, 2008 01:22 PM, CST
We are still enjoying life at home. I will say, I forgot just how busy the school year is around here. I really am trying to create a new normal with all we have learned

since last November. If I start my day with even just a few minutes focusing on God, asking Him to direct my steps, thoughts, and words, my family and I all benefit greatly. Leaving Him out of the equation never works.

MONDAY, OCTOBER 27, 2008 11:46 AM, CST

These last weeks have been wonderful. Jack is feeling well and really enjoying the days he is able to go to school. He has quite a bit of new, soft, hair! Just yesterday he was out front playing football with some neighborhood boys. They are all a few years older, but are so good with him—even complimentary of how he can truly keep up with them. Last week I joined his class for a field trip to the pumpkin patch. It was good for him to go . . . feeling well this year. He reminds us that during the trip last year he was trying to tell us he was sick, but that we did not understand. He is correct. I just cannot express how it feels to watch him enjoy himself, doing the activities a four year old should be doing. The treatment of cancer is so painful. His is not over yet, but I can assuredly tell you this . . . Jack Huffman's healing to date is a miracle. Being a part of his, has allowed us to recognize others that we previously would have overlooked. I am so thankful for every moment (even the less charming) with him, with all of our family. Soon after Jack was diagnosed, (after several "Sally Field" moments, and experiencing pain I did not know existed) I shared with a friend that I feel he is, just as Harold and Elizabeth are to me, gifts from God. Our family may have him with us for four years, or ninety-four. We will love, nurture, and enjoy him for as long as we are allowed on earth—then for an eternity in heaven. God has taught us so much, and healed us as well, through this journey with our sweet Jack. We may not understand all of His ways, but we do not need to. We trust Him. Your prayers help us to strengthen and maintain our trust.

As the ebb and flow continued, Molly Beth continued to amaze me with her insight and faith. She wrote, "As real and painful as much of our year has been, the beauty that only our Lord could provide through it is much more powerful."

Another tumor was discovered, this time in Jack's chest. He was also battling with a bout of pneumonia through the radiation to try and shrink the new growth. Molly Beth wrote, "I am unabashedly asking you to be on your knees for Jack."

A CT scan revealed that the tumor was growing and there was possibly bone involvement. The chemotherapy didn't appear to be helping Jack, but Molly Beth confirmed the doctors were doing everything within their power. It was time to dig deep and call out to God.

A friend in Greenville suggested a twenty-four-hour prayer vigil for Jack, Molly Beth, Harold, and Elizabeth. Although Jack was covered with prayer all the time, the intentional designated time was an inspirational and beautiful idea.

: : : : : :

The flame continued to dance.

As I stood in the circle holding hands, sweaty palms and all, I just wanted to know that this gathering of the brokenhearted would work. I wanted the little flame to erupt like a column of raging fire as seen in a Steven Spielberg movie. Better yet, a pillar of God's presence from the Ark of the Covenant straight up to heaven with Jack and me on the top of it. It would take us right up to the front door of God's house. With a gentle rap on the door, God would answer.

"Yes, can I help you?" God would say.

"Why, yes You can," I would answer. "You see, Jack, this little boy here . . ."

Of course God would interrupt me before I could get it out because God is God. He is all-knowing. He knows what we want, what we need, what we are going to say and do. He is God.

So we would end up just looking at each other, with me holding Jack's hand and Jack holding Caroline Bear wearing a Spiderman outfit. God would not say a word. He would just touch Jack's tummy and all the cancer would be gone. Jack and I would ride the pillar of the blazing spirit of God back down to the hospital and I would trumpet the good news—Jack is cured! God healed him!

That's what I wanted. That's what we all wanted.

Instead, my doubts and cynicism overwhelmed me. *This séance is about us. To make us feel better. How are our pleadings and prayers going to help this situation?* I pondered. *The doctors think they have found more cancer and it's spreading.* I couldn't help but feel hopeless.

A younger Gene would have made fun of this prayer nonsense, I thought. *It will never work. These people are crazy.*

But my heart was again struck. *This will work. We have the power to call out directly to our Savior! Our prayers are all we have now.*

After a brief introduction from one of our pastors, the prayers began, one by one in the circle. My wife started. Mary sat in the inner circle.

She took a deep breath, "God, please help Jack . . ."

The tears could be heard falling in the still of the room with every prayer to God.

With each squeeze of the hand the next person offered up a cry to God. Then the next, then the next, then the next. My daughter Caroline ended the inner circle with a beautiful and heart-wrenching pleading.

My turn.

I hope my prayer works, I thought in reluctant doubt. *But it's hard to believe my words could make a difference.*

Over 100 prayers to God. Surely He had to hear some of them or at least one of them.

Now, just as the Huffman family was so accustomed to doing, we waited. We waited on the status of the scan, of the tests, of Jack's fate. How could God take away what the doctors saw a few days ago? Could He make it just disappear?

> WEDNESDAY, JANUARY 28, 2009 08:46 AM, CST
> Jack's bone scan was CLEAR! The CT showed "slight improvement" with the tumor.
> I believe you all know the "stats" for not only a diagnosis of Neuroblastoma, but also a relapse. Perhaps at this point, we are all realizing the Power at work in our midst. While healing this boy, God is working in our community, our families, our hearts. Thank you for the twenty-four hour prayers, and the beautiful gathering Sunday. Incredible.

What was I thinking? After this unbelievable news I had to re-think my thinking. Of course there is this healing God. Of course He heard our prayers. My problem with the doubts I felt were doubts of the head and not doubts of the heart. The head doubts are natural. Our rational human selves want to override the truth of the heart. Sure God is concerned about the head, but He is more concerned with the condition of our hearts.

The fact was that what the doctors thought they saw was no longer there. Twenty-four hours of prayer and an intense prayer session, and the spots were gone. We stepped on the pillar of fire and knocked at God's door.

By no means did this mean Jack was back to the young, cancer-free, rambunctious boy of summer 2007. There were still challenges, still procedures, still tests, and still more of the same process that people with cancer have to deal with. But it was a step, a healing step. I believe God looked into our collective hearts and absorbed the love we had for little Jack and used it to ease the pain and suffering, even if it was temporary. Molly Beth confirmed our connection with God when she wrote, "We continue to find strength in His Spirit which is in each one of us. Your prayers are an enormous gift and completely encouraging."

The battle was won, but the war raged on.

TUESDAY, FEBRUARY 17, 2009 06:02 AM, CST
... I feel I must close with a scripture that has been on my mind. The night before last, I desperately wanted to find this particular one ... I could only remember the beginning, and needed to read it in its entirety. After about an hour, I decided to just read my devotions and go to sleep. I opened the first book, and there it was, Ephesians 3:20–21. I smiled and read it of course. Still smiling, I opened the second book, and there it was, Ephesians 3:20–21. Now glory be to God who by his mighty power at work within us is able to do far more than we would ever dare to ask or even dream of—infinitely beyond our highest prayers, desires, thoughts, or hopes. May He be given glory forever and ever ...

FRIDAY, FEBRUARY 27, 2009 02:25 PM, CST

As I held Jack's head, wiped his nose and mouth, and reassured him, he stated between bouts of sickness, "I don't want to do this anymore." I heard the cry come from my mouth. It was to the One who has been with Jack, with us, all along. He is faithful. Jack, by this time, was enduring his third episode of vomiting blood so at 3am Thursday morning we headed on to the hospital.

. . . As I believe there are no coincidences, yesterday during my reading, words from the hymn "My Grace is Sufficient for Thee" were provided, as well as Psalm 63:1–8. Last night, before going to sleep I decided to read one more devotion . . . the scripture at the top of the page read . . . "My grace is sufficient for thee."

. . . I am finally filling out the paperwork for Jack's wish trip . . . Disney of course. We are thinking about going over the Thanksgiving break . . . I'll keep you posted . . . Before I close, I would like to share one more moment from this week. As Jack lifted his shirt for port accessing, he commented on the fact the he has a lot of scars. He does—across his tummy, his upper left chest, down the center and across his chest, his back, and a few little ones scattered about. Every time I see them it reminds me that all of those times—scary, dark, painful times—have led to deeper joy while watching the smile on his face as he walks up the steps at school. And that the hand we grip throughout all of these times, the hand guiding us, and leading him up those steps, has scars too—and in His feet, and scattered about. I am so thankful I can barely keep my composure.

Having that said, Harold and I are well aware of who Jack's Healer is. We continue to trust Him to lead us, our doctors, and use the illness He has allowed for good, and for His glory.

The war still raged on.

MONDAY, MAY 17, 2010 9:53 AM, CST
Jack's last scans did show disease progression, and he received some chemotherapy about two weeks ago. . . . This helped to reduce his pain, but also his weight. . . . We should be back home tomorrow, and be able to continue this through home health. At this point, our plans are to continue with one more round of this chemotherapy as we wait to see if he is eligible for the ALK study. We continue to pray ceaselessly with thanksgiving, and for continued guidance and strength. Thank you so much for your ongoing support for Jack, and our family.

Six days later.

SUNDAY, MAY 23, 2010 9:40 AM, CST
To God be the Glory, He has restored Jack and made him whole again. To God be the Glory, He welcomed our sweet Jack into the kingdom of heaven last night. Though our hearts ache and we are hurting, we trust in His promise that we will see Jack and hold Jack when one day we reunite.

: : : : : :

The courage and faith displayed by Molly Beth and Harold was mind-boggling. I could never quite grasp how they clutched the slippery handle of faith in the face of ceaseless terror and doubt. For 31 months, they never questioned the love, peace, and resolve found in the lap of God. For 31 months, they taught us how to depend on Him. For 31 months, they set the standard for how we should thank and love our Father in times of distress.

Jack's short life was a gift to us all. His parents' faith in their time of trouble was a resounding example of courage as they taught us how we should always trust in God and accept His plan for our life, even if it is not our plan. Jack's life taught us that every day is truly precious and that every waking moment, good and bad, is a gift. It taught us that only God knows whether we are on this earth for six years or ninety-six. It reminded us of the pain God must have felt when His only Son, the teacher of man, died on the splintered cross.

It reminded us that we are all called to teach our brothers and sisters that God is real and always there for us in our darkest and most fearful days.

Jack's fragile life was a gleaming ray of light into our day. He showed us that even a three-year-old boy could be our teacher. Jack Huffman taught us how to live.

When God Talks

*"God told me to strike at al Qaida and I struck them,
and then he instructed me to strike at Saddam, which I did,
and now I am determined to solve the problem in the Middle East.
If you help me I will act, and if not,
the elections will come and I will have to focus on them."*
—GEORGE W. BUSH[18]

IT HAS ALWAYS DISTRESSED ME when people say God told them to do something.

"Why would you say something like that?" I'd question. "You can't hear God's voice booming from the sky. I just don't believe it."

In fact, I could go as far as calling someone crazy and boldly suggesting it was time for them to check in. It simply made no sense that God could or would talk directly to people. I gave in to the concept that it happened four thousand years ago as told in the Bible. For example, God spoke to Moses and Aaron in the book of Exodus:

> The LORD said to Moses and Aaron in Egypt, "This month is to be for you the first month, the first month of your year. Tell the whole community of Israel that on the tenth day of this month each man is to take a lamb for his family, one for each household. If any household is too small for a whole lamb, they must share one with their nearest neighbor, having taken into account the number

of people there are. You are to determine the amount of lamb needed in accordance with what each person will eat. The animals you choose must be year-old males without defect, and you may take them from the sheep or the goats. Take care of them until the fourteenth day of the month, when all the members of the community of Israel must slaughter them at twilight. Then they are to take some of the blood and put it on the sides and tops of the doorframes of the houses where they eat the lambs. That same night they are to eat the meat roasted over the fire, along with bitter herbs, and bread made without yeast. Do not eat the meat raw or boiled in water, but roast it over a fire—with the head, legs and internal organs. Do not leave any of it till morning; if some is left till morning, you must burn it. This is how you are to eat it: with your cloak tucked into your belt, your sandals on your feet and your staff in your hand. Eat it in haste; it is the LORD's Passover."[19]

Wow. That seems to be a fairly detailed recollection of God's voice. For all I know it was verbatim. Still, that's a pretty direct and specific list of instructions. But okay, it's acceptable. I believe God spoke to Moses and Aaron.

I even accept the fact that God spoke directly to Paul, a horrible sinner transformed into a warrior for God two thousand years ago as described in 2 Corinthians: "Three times I pleaded with the Lord to take it away from me. But he said to me, 'My grace is sufficient for you, for my power is made perfect in weakness.'"[20]

Okay. I'm in. However, I could never accept that it happened yesterday, today, or will happen in the future.

Give me a break.

Conversations with God appear to have become a regular occurrence with the common man. Too many people have used the veil of a connection with God to either support their position, endorse their cause, or make an excuse for their actions.

The controversial pastor, Jim Baker, once said that God told him to build a "Christian Disneyland" in the Charlotte area. After Baker's empire crumbled like a chunk of stale cornbread, it was clear his position was to support his own desire for cash, opulence, and the dream to reign over his loyal flock with lies and sexual perversions.

Countless murderers claimed that God told them to commit manslaughter or heinous acts as a defense for their actions: "God told me to rape, torture, mutilate, and kill that seven-year-old girl." I don't think so.

The Father also allegedly talks to the most well-intentioned people. "God spoke to me and told me I should make a library for my church," said Frances Grigsby. "I had all these boxes of books that wasn't doing anybody any good, they were just sitting there. God told me that this was something I could do to help others and hopefully get more young people interested in coming to the church."[21]

Who am I to doubt that God told Frances to make a library? I just want to know if it was in a loud voice, a dream, a whisper, or a letter in the mailbox.

It's more complicated to discount when Molly Beth told me that she heard her son, Jack, clearly talking to someone while in his hospital bed. Unfortunately, she couldn't make out what he was saying just hours before he breathed his last breath on this earth. She believed he was having a conversation with God. Oddly enough, that was believable in addition to offering immense comfort to a grieving mother.

Nonetheless, the concept of God talking to us in our normal daily life is outrageous! But who am I to say that God does or doesn't talk directly to people?

: : : : : :

The virgin snow drifted outside the window of my cozy hotel room. As the minutes passed, the snow picked up and fell in heavy snowball-making clumps. There is always something magical about snow and how it silently floats from heaven to earth. A March snow was getting late in the winter season even for Saratoga Springs, New York.

I had just arrived for a conference and an awards ceremony, traveling directly from a business convention in Chicago. I was tired, road-weary, and playing host to an extraordinary sinus infection. I just wanted to get undressed, get in bed, and fall asleep with the sneaker screeching of the ACC Basketball Tournament easing from the TV.

I arrived late so the conference was already well underway. I wanted to sleep. Since my main purpose was to attend the event for the awards ceremony, I figured I wouldn't miss much if I skipped a few sessions.

I slipped into the warm bed.

I was restless. I could easily fall asleep but I felt a nudge to get up and go listen to the keynote speaker for the day. I didn't want to move from my sanctuary but I felt an abnormal urge to get up from my comfortable bed and hear the speaker.

"Okay," I said to myself. "Let me at least look in the program to see who is speaking."

Dr. Walter J. Turnbull, founder of the Boys Choir of Harlem, the brochure read.

I was familiar with the Boys Choir but didn't really think he had anything special to tell me. *What's he gonna say that I don't already know?* I thought boastfully. *They are a choir from New York that sings around the world and they help educate kids too. I know how his tale ends.* It was your standard do-good-in-the-hood story.

I went back to bed.

I stayed restless. I felt compelled to go hear him, listen to him, although I didn't want to. Something battled within me. The clash rang in my head, *Should I stay or should I go?*

Whether it was guilt or God's hand nudging me out of bed, I got dressed and joined the other 300 people in the auditorium.

Dr. Turnbull weaved his extraordinary saga of struggle and perseverance together into a beautiful journey of hope and healing. It was a story of taking risks and saving lives. He captivated me. He brought me to tears.

At one point in his story, it was as if all time stopped. I couldn't hear Dr. Turnbull speak anymore and the people next to me froze. It seemed like a shot of light cleared my mind and planted a vivid picture of what my future would hold. It showed me that I was going to represent the Boys Choir of Harlem on a global stage. Ah-ha! It was an epiphany! I referred to it as a moment of clarity.

Ordinarily, I wouldn't have had a chance at signing the Boys Choir of Harlem to a client sponsorship and music representation agreement. I would be a white guy from a semi-rural area in the South representing a black organization from the middle of Harlem, the hood. What made it even more challenging was that this was at the same time that the state of South Carolina was fighting its own civil war about whether or not to take the rebel flag down from the top of the state house dome. Many organizations had already come out and banned relationships with South Carolina as well as implement boycotts ceasing doing business within the state. We were a white company from rebel flag-flying South Carolina; we were worlds apart. It didn't seem to matter, the image was clear, I saw what I saw, I felt what I felt, and I heard what I heard.

His words picked up and the people next to me moved in their chairs: real time again.

He finished his speech and, as most speeches end, he was swarmed by vocal inquisitors trying to glean a bit of greatness and direction from the person delivering the powerful message. I rarely did that.

I sprinted to the front of the room like Carl Lewis battling for a gold medal. This time, I was first in line.

"Dr. Turnbull," I said, gasping for breath. "My name is Gene Krcelic. I will make this short; I know a lot of people want to talk to you. Does the Boys Choir have any sponsors? I mean do you actively sell sponsorships?" Much of my work background had a component of sponsorship sales associated with it and I had quite a bit of success in that area.

"Not really," he answered. "We have done a little in the past but not nearly what we should be doing."

"Do you mind if I get your card? I would love to follow up with you about sponsorship sales for your organization."

"Sure, I'd love to talk to you about it."

"Thank you," I said as he handed me his card. "Also, could I please have your name tag?"

He looked at me with a slow twist of his head at the request for the plastic-covered piece of paper pinned to his lapel. He took it off and handed it to me without a word.

"Thank you."

When I opened the door to my room, I felt different. I wasn't as tired or weary. My sinus infection was on the mend and I was revived with a sense of purpose. I had vividly understood and taken action in my moment of clarity. "I got this. I will sign the Boys Choir of Harlem."

: : : : : :

The awards ceremony culminated with the Prism Award, an honor given to the organization that exemplified the most creative artistic programming in the world for First Night Celebrations, an artistic non-alcoholic New Year's Eve event. I was the executive director for the one in Greenville. An employee had submitted our project for the award after she had creatively conceived the idea.

We were one of five finalists.

The banquet hall was dark and only illuminated by stage lighting and the small candles on each of the round dinner tables. Three hundred people anxiously awaited the final honors so the DJ could start spinning the tunes and the dancing could begin. Although it was an award only a relatively small number of people cared about, it was extremely important for those people in the room. I was abnormally nervous. I liked winning. Winning was always better than losing, an unfortunate result of my ultra-competitive nature.

The crowd was hushed as the final announcement neared.

I was sweaty and anxious.

"The winner of this year's Prism Award is . . . First Night Greenville."

Wow! I thought. *I can't believe it—we won! Yes!*

My weak knees carried me to the podium. I was humbled. I delivered the standard thank-yous and gave the proper credit for the award.

With a quiet room and a captive audience I had the opportunity to recall our speaker from earlier in the day. I had the chance to make a lasting impression.

"This afternoon we heard from Dr. Walter Turnbull," I began. "He is a man who picked cotton in the fields of Mississippi, marched and fought through the civil rights movement with Dr. Martin Luther King Jr.; he relocated to New York City and cleaned public toilets to pay for his books so he could attend music school. Dr. Turnbull then started an organization in the basement of a church to help inner-city kids break the cycle of poor education and do it in a revolutionary and radical way, through music. He fought against all odds and achieved greatness, not for him but for the underprivileged children he so loved. The Boys and Girls Choirs of Harlem now perform before presidents and kings all over this world. They are the benchmark for revolution in creating a sustainable and life-altering education program. He is a man with unparalleled drive and perseverance to overcome every obstacle in his life. Dr. Walter Turnbull is a champion."

I reached into my jacket pocket, pulled out his nametag, and held it in the air.

"I asked him for his nametag today. I am going to frame it and put it on my wall so I can look at it every day and let it serve as a symbol of being able to overcome every obstacle in my life. When we have so much to do in a given day and the calls are piling up, re-member the Boys Choir of Harlem. When people are complaining because things aren't going as planned, think about Walter Turnbull. When you feel you have no more energy and it's just too hard to go on and the obstacles in your life are just way too overwhelming, think of this name tag and what it represents. It represents a man we can all look up to, a man we can all learn from, a true American hero. Walter Turnbull is my inspiration. Thank you."

There was a brief silence.

The applause started and each person, one by one, began to stand and clap. It was like a rolling wave from table to table. I was taken aback at the response.

Before the DJ started to play, two young ladies from Idaho stopped me on my way back to my table.

"Can I have your name tag?" one of them said.

I was shocked. I was momentarily speechless. "Why do you want *my* nametag?" I asked in utter humility.

"Because you are going to be our inspiration. Your artistic project has motivated us to create something great, and we are going to win this award next year."

I really didn't know what to say. For one of the rare moments in my life I was at a complete loss for words. I always deeply enjoyed handing out compliments and offering praise to others; however, it always made me oddly uncomfortable when a compliment was dished out in my direction.

I wanted to inspire others by the journey of Dr. Turnbull; I had no intention of being someone else's inspiration. That was a lot of responsibility. In retrospect, it taught me that God not only talks to people directly, He uses our unique talents to talk through us, to communicate to others in any way that will be heard.

For a brief moment Satan had me trapped in a hotel room with no motivation to go and listen to the person that would change the course of my life and my business. God won the battle and not only sent me to hear a man that would change my life but used me to change the lives of others. At the moment, it was easy to say it was me doing these simple yet extraordinary things. Only hindsight offered the gift of the true revelation, revealing to me that it was God at work, not me.

By listening to God's voice, even though I didn't know it was Him at the time, I was led to sign the Boys Choir of Harlem as a client, against all odds. I created the global sponsorship program for their organization and developed a mainstream recording project from the talent-rich choir. Those projects led me into relationships within the New York and Los Angeles music scenes that I would have never had the chance to penetrate. When a representative from the Boys Choir of Harlem called, people answered the phone. As the dots later connected, those relationships placed me in the position where I could drastically change people's lives for His glory.

Over the subsequent year, First Night Greenville was filled with a passion to do something even greater and try to win the award for an unprecedented second consecutive year. We developed a program that taught blind people how to sculpt with clay. When we exhibited the pieces of art, we had them displayed in a dark tent. Before the public could experience the exhibit, each person was blindfolded and could only view the artwork with their hands. We rationalized that since the pieces were created in the dark they could only be experienced in the dark.

One of the blind artists wrote, "An obstacle that I have overcome was my fear of water. It took me three times to get used to it. Now I am not afraid anymore. I am now fascinated by deep water. NO FEAR . . . GO YOUR LIMITS."

Winning the award became insignificant compared to changing that one person's life and hearing of her resulting truth—no fear.

Our project didn't make the finals as in the prior year; nonetheless I went to the conference and the awards ceremony. The winning project was truly spectacular. During the winner's acceptance speech, she noted that our winning project from the year before had inspired their project. She said it challenged them to create something larger than life and truly make an enormous impact. They credited us for their inspiration. God was still clearly at work once more.

I was humbled and uncomfortable again.

: : : : : :

In real time, it is often hard to realize what is actually happening when something monumental is occurring. When that moment of clarity takes place, it's easy to ignore that it's God Who is talking to your heart in a truly unique way. It's easy to say, "Hey, look at me, I just figured it out." It's easy to avoid looking deep enough to realize that we had nothing to do with it at all. It wasn't until I had true oneness with God that I realized on a cold March day in Upstate New York, God spoke to me in a way that I would accept. He said, "Get out of that bed and go." He nudged me to get out from those warm, comfortable sheets while Satan tried to keep me where I was. They fought. God later used Dr. Turnbull's words to stop the world for *my moment of clarity*, or rather *God's moment of clarity*. They continued to fight, but God won.

I have come to firmly believe that God talks to us every day. He speaks through moments of clarity, through a brisk autumn breeze, through the actions and words of others, in our dreams, and even in a loud and audible, booming voice. Who am I to say how God chooses to communicate with people? I can only testify how He communicated with me.

Many Christians opt to say "Gold told me to" or "God said." I like to think God shows me and communicates with me however I can best see His plan for my life. Everyone is different; thus, everyone needs to be communicated with in a unique way that suits their acceptance. He reveals His voice to whomever He wants, whenever He wants, however He wants. Whether or not people are truthful about their communications with God, that is up to them and they will be judged for it.

I now know the best way to see and hear how God speaks to us: be aware that He *is* speaking to us. For so many years He communicated to me but I never knew it. I wasn't looking for His movement in my life. My eyes were covered, my ears were plugged, and my heart was in chains. Now that my heart is free and I can hear and see God's movement, I am aware He is answering my daily questions. God is clear and intentional. The answers to all of my questions are right in front of me at all times; I simply need to be prepared to accept them. He is everywhere.

I believe God talks. My prayer is that I will keep listening to God's voice and know the difference when He stops talking and when I foolishly try to complete His sentence for Him.

Let's Go Back to God

Give me Words to speak
Don't let my Spirit sleep
Cause I can't think of anything worth saying
But I know that I owe You my life
So give me Words to speak
Don't let my Spirit sleep.
—Aaron Shust[22]

TRIUNE MERCY CENTER IS A non-denominational mission church that ministers with and alongside the homeless. It serves both marginalized and affluent Christians. In other words, it serves both those living in big houses and those without houses. Triune serves the homeless by providing emergency relief services such as hot meals, groceries, clothes, drug rehab referrals, and other essentials.

As a deacon in my church, I was named the chair of the committee that served Triune. I knew nothing about it other than knowing the pastor who ran the community ministry. She was a successful businesswoman who quit her job, went into seminary, and was called to lead in a ministerial capacity. She didn't get the call to lead a posh church serving the rich and famous. Her call was to serve the homeless: ground zero. It was the very place where Jesus would most likely be found—not in a million-dollar church with stained glass windows, but in a soup kitchen healing and feeding His flock.

This was where my church and God put me. My responsibility was to rally church members as volunteers to feed the homeless on a quarterly basis. At first, my volunteers were thin in numbers, but by the time my three-year term ended, I had recruited nearly one hundred volunteers contributing over three hundred volunteer hours.

Deb, the saint who ran Triune, was always there, faithful, and diligent. She served as a leader, a mother, a mentor, and whatever else God needed her to represent. After the Sunday dinners she would lead a church service for the homeless and anyone else who cared to worship God in their humble sanctuary. It was real. Those with homes filled the front wooden pews. Those who slept in the abandoned buildings, under the bridges, on the sidewalks, or in the bamboo thicket chose to sit in the back.

: : : : : :

God blesses each and every one of us with talents, skills we can use in our everyday life. But with each of God's blessings there are always deficiencies in other areas. Some of the most talented humans suffer deep deficiencies. Mozart was a brilliant composer, writing music at a tender age when most children haven't even started school. Even with his enormous gift of composing music, he was plagued with intolerable social skills. Albert Einstein. He was one of the most advanced and brilliant minds of the twentieth century; however, he suffered from early speech and learning challenges. Stephen Hawking. Another unparalleled mind of our generation has been confined to a wheel chair as a paraplegic and has written some of the most highly developed theories on space that mankind has ever read. And he wrote much of his work tapping out the words on a keyboard with a stick in his mouth, one letter at a time.

God gives, God takes away.

Although I feel I am blessed with strong common sense, I lack traditional book sense. I feel I am blessed with the talent of communicating and public speaking; however, there are times when I get overconfident in my own ability and say things that come out wrong—good intentions gone awry. God gives each of us a raw talent that we must hone and use to glorify and please Him.

There had always been an aching in my soul to deliver a sermon, even though I lacked any reasonable qualification. Without any formal ministry training, the reality of standing in front of a congregation and delivering God's Word or a spiritual message was just a faint dream. In high school my shelf was filled with public speaking competition awards, and I had plenty of experience speaking at conventions and seminars around the world, but a sermon was just a faint dream.

When Deb called and asked me how my public speaking was, there was no lack of confidence. "I'm pretty good," I said with my usual egocentric manner.

"How would you like to deliver the message on Sunday, October 26 at 6:00 p.m.?"

I wasn't sure what I had just heard. If my brain processed it correctly, she had just asked me to deliver the sermon at her church.

"I would love to. I'm honored that you would ask. I hope I don't let you down." I was dumbstruck. *What did I just agree to do?*

: : : : : :

Triune Mercy Center is an old church. The sanctuary is simple and beautiful.

During the Sunday evening service, the makeshift choir of whoever wants to stand around the piano and sing creates a cacophony of God's voices. The performance won't win an American Idol audition, but I'm sure God smiles with every chorus.

I sat on the front pew waiting for my introduction. As I sat I sweated. Butterflies danced in my lower intestine. Anxiety grew.

What do I think I'm doing? I thought as my feeble mind raced. *How am I qualified to deliver a message to the people in this historic room? What in the world am I doing here?*

I looked behind me at the faces in the pews. I saw people without a home and others who live in million-dollar homes. I saw dirty, ragged clothing and immaculate outfits. I saw zero-aires and I saw millionaires. *How in the world am I going to be able to communicate the message I prepared for this most diverse group of people?* I thought.

I wanted out.

I thought, *Okay, I'm going to just go off the top of my head and throw away my scripted message.* It was sitting neatly on my lap in a manila folder.

No.

Yes.

No. My anxiety was getting the best of me.

The time was drawing near.

Gene, just read it. Maintain eye contact and trust that God gives you the strength and composure to deliver a meaningful message. I just hoped my knees would support me as I walked up to the microphone.

"Delivering our message today is Gene Krcelic," Deb said after the hymn.

Well, there's no turning back now, I said as I inhaled a deep breath. I composed myself and opened my mouth:

Hope.

We all want inspiration from our leaders . . . we all want hope. We want hope from the leaders of our churches, companies, and we want leadership and hope from our president.

What a chance. What an opportunity to deliver a message to a group of people with less than ten days before a presidential election where we select the leader of our country. Perhaps I should try to sway your vote to my side of the table; maybe I'll scare you into voting for my guy because your guy has way too many issues, too many incomplete plans for the future of our country. He has NO plan to help ME. You see, my guy will help you feel secure in your house in the dead of winter, that is if you have a house. If you have no place to stay he'll give you peace of mind for better times ahead. He's the one with all the answers. After watching the debates, it only solidified my position. There's no doubt about it, my guy is the guy.

We need some straight talk ... some real talk ... no rhetoric but truth! Let's take a look back over a few thousand years and hear what some of the great leaders said when they had their moment to shine, to address the masses. Four leaders and the words they used to inspire ... to give hope.

How about Moses? He chose to quote God directly as the messenger of God's Word, although Moses was a leader in his own right. He was leading 600,000 men plus women plus children out of Egypt. That's about a million people strong. So around 1400 BC this is what Moses said, according to the English Standard Version:

God told me to tell you ... and I quote: "I am the LORD your God, who brought you out of the land of Egypt, out of the house of slavery.

You shall have no other gods before me.

You shall not make for yourself a carved image, or any likeness of anything that is in heaven above, or that is in the earth beneath, or that is in the water under the earth. You shall not bow down to them or serve them, for I the LORD your God am a jealous God. . . .

You shall not take the name of the LORD your God in vain. . . .
Remember the Sabbath day, to keep it holy. . . .
Honor your father and your mother. . . .
You shall not murder.
You shall not commit adultery.
You shall not steal.
You shall not bear false witness against your neighbor.
You shall not covet your neighbor's house; you shall not covet
your neighbor's wife, or his male servant, or his female servant,
or his ox, or his donkey, or anything that is your neighbor's."

Now that's straight talk! Straight faith! Straight obedience. He lived the words! No rhetoric . . . just the Truth.

Let's fast forward about 1,427 years. Another great leader speaks . . . the greatest leader to ever grace planet earth. This must have been a scene . . . Jesus walking along the hillside near the Sea of Galilee; His closest disciples around Him followed by a mass of clamoring humanity . . . about 5,000 strong. Imagine this: you're sitting in your office on Main Street or waiting for the bus on Pendleton Street and a man walks by followed by 5,000 people. People are saying he's going down to Reedy River Park and he's going to give everyone a message, a message that will save mankind. What are you going to do? I know what I'm doing—I'm going to join the crowd and find out what this guy is going to say.

Matthew tells us from his perspective what Jesus said. Here are some excerpts of straight talk from that day found in Matthew 5, 6, and 7. So there they are, Jesus getting ready to give the speech of a lifetime:

And he opened his mouth and taught them, saying:
"Blessed are the poor in spirit, for theirs is the kingdom of heaven.
Blessed are those who mourn, for they shall be comforted.
Blessed are the meek, for they shall inherit the earth.

Blessed are those who hunger and thirst for righteousness, for they shall be satisfied.

Blessed are the merciful, for they shall receive mercy.

Blessed are the pure in heart, for they shall see God.

Blessed are the peacemakers, for they shall be called sons of God.

Blessed are those who are persecuted for righteousness' sake, for theirs is the kingdom of heaven. . . .

Do not think that I have come to abolish the Law or the Prophets; I have not come to abolish them but to fulfill them."

Jesus goes on to talk about things such as murder, adultery, and love. He challenges His disciples to think about and respond to those human acts in new and revolutionary ways. Jesus continues,

"No one can serve two masters. . . . You cannot serve God and money. . . .

Therefore do not be anxious about tomorrow, for tomorrow will be anxious for itself. Sufficient for the day is its own trouble. . . .

Ask, and it will be given to you; seek, and you will find; knock, and it will be opened to you. For everyone who asks receives, and the one who seeks finds, and to the one who knocks it will be opened."

Jesus concludes the Sermon on the Mount:

"Everyone then who hears these words of mine and does them will be like a wise man who built his house on the rock. And the rain fell, and the floods came, and the winds blew and beat on that house, but it did not fall, because it had been founded on the rock. And everyone who hears these words of mine and does not do them will be like a foolish man who built his house on the sand. And the rain fell, and the floods came, and the winds blew and beat against that house, and it fell, and great was the fall of it."

Straight talk.

No rhetoric . . . the Truth.

He lived the words! He died for these words! He is the Word.

Now let's fast forward again 1,836 years: Perhaps one of the greatest presidents in our country's young history, Abraham Lincoln, gives a short but riveting address in the dedication of the Soldiers' National Cemetery in Gettysburg, Pennsylvania . . . perhaps the greatest speech in United States history. Here's a sample for consideration:

> *Four score and seven years ago our fathers brought forth on this continent, a new nation, conceived in Liberty, and dedicated to the proposition that all men are created equal. . . .*
>
> *The world will little note, nor long remember what we say here, but it can never forget what they did here. It is for us the living, rather, to be dedicated here to the unfinished work which they who fought here have thus far so nobly advanced. It is rather for us to be here dedicated to the great task remaining before us— that from these honored dead we take increased devotion to that cause for which they gave the last full measure of devotion—that we here highly resolve that these dead shall not have died in vain—that this nation, under God, shall have a new birth of freedom—and that government of the people, by the people, for the people, shall not perish from the earth.*[23]

Straight talk.

No rhetoric . . . the Truth.

A call to action. He lived the words! He died for these words.

Whatever happened to great words from great men? Memorable words from memorable men? What do people say when they have a chance to influence . . . a chance to lead, a chance to change our human condition?

Forward 100 years: August 28, 1963, Washington DC.

A revolutionary man trying to reform America. A Moses in his own right, leading his people out of bondage. A King. Martin Luther King Jr.

I heard a voice shout, "I knew it, I knew it!"

Here's an excerpt from his straight talk:

> We have also come to this hallowed spot to remind America of the fierce urgency of Now. . . . Now is the time to lift our nation from the quicksands of racial injustice to the solid rock of brotherhood. Now is the time to make justice a reality for all of God's children. . . .
>
> Go back to Mississippi, go back to Alabama, go back to South Carolina, go back to Georgia, go back to Louisiana, go back to the slums and ghettos of our northern cities, knowing that somehow this situation can and will be changed.
>
> Let us not wallow in the valley of despair, I say to you today, my friends.
>
> And so even though we face the difficulties of today and tomorrow, I still have a dream. It is a dream deeply rooted in the American dream.
>
> I have a dream that one day this nation will rise up and live out the true meaning of its creed: "We hold these truths to be self-evident, that all men are created equal."
>
> . . . I have a dream that my four little children will one day live in a nation where they will not be judged by the color of their skin but by the content of their character.
>
> I have a dream today!

He goes on.

I have a dream that one day every valley shall be exalted, and every hill and mountain shall be made low, the rough places will be made plain, and the crooked places will be made straight; "and the glory of the Lord shall be revealed and all flesh shall see it together."

I began to hear some "Amens" and "Hallelujahs" emerge from the congregation.

This is our hope, and this is the faith that I go back to the South with.

. . . With this faith, we will be able to work together, to pray together, to struggle together, to go to jail together, to stand up for freedom together, knowing that we will be free one day.

. . . And if America is to be a great nation, this must become true. And so let freedom ring from the prodigious hilltops of New Hampshire.

. . . Let freedom ring from Stone Mountain of Georgia.

My voice grew louder.

And when this happens, when we allow freedom ring, when we let it ring from every village and every hamlet, from every state and every city, we will be able to speed up that day when all of God's children, black men and white men, Jews and Gentiles, Protestants and Catholics, will be able to join hands and sing in the words of the old Negro spiritual:
Free at last! Free at last!

I heard clapping reign from the middle of the congregation.

Thank God Almighty, we are free at last![24]

Now that's a contemporary leader.

Straight talk.

No rhetoric . . . words of Truth with a vivid passion for God!

He lived the words! He died for these words.

What in the world ever happened to great, memorable words? Martin Luther King Jr., Abraham Lincoln, Jesus, Moses, God . . . Let's go back to God.

One more bit of straight talk . . . I was telling you about MY guy, you know, the one with all the answers, the one I'm voting for . . . to me it's absolutely clear as a handful of raindrops.

You know who I'm talking about. . . .

I'm voting for God.

You see, God is the only one that's going to get us out of this mess that we got ourselves into. . . . Let's go back to God.

In the beginning God created the heavens and the earth and it was good, God said let there be light and it was good, God said let there be sky, let there be water, let there be land, and it was good. Let there be vegetation, living creatures in the waters, winged birds in the sky, living creatures on the land, and it was good. . . . Let's go back to God.

Then God said let us make man and let them rule over all the creatures of the earth . . . man in God's own image . . . man and woman. And God said it was good, very good! God made it perfect, so on the seventh day He rested. . . . Let's go back to God.

God did a pretty good job, if you ask me. So what went wrong? Why is this world heading for a state of depression? Why is the cost of living so high? Why are there wars with people dying for no apparent reason? Why can't we provide adequate healthcare for every single American? Why are some children being left without an education? Why is it so costly to put gas in your car . . . if you have a car? Why do you have to sleep under a bridge at night? Why is food so expensive? Why are things so bad? Why is it so hard to love? . . . Why? . . . Why? . . . Why? Let's go back to God.

The question why may seem tough, but the answer is quite simple. Because man thought we could do it better than God . . . we can carry on without God. "Hey, God, don't worry about it . . . we got it from here!" The fact of the matter is without God . . . there is nothing . . . nothing . . . Let's go back to God.

Here is my two-part challenge, a call to action. Number one: Go and vote a week from Tuesday and cast a ballot for the next president of the United States of America . . . however you opt to exercise your right, it doesn't matter to me, just vote.

Number two: . . . saving the best for last . . . Vote for the only One that can get us out of this mess we got ourselves into. And here's the beautiful part of this: you don't even need to be registered to vote. But here's the deal, don't wait for the first Tuesday in November to cast your ballot. Vote now. Vote today. Vote every day. Vote with every breath you've been blessed with. Vote for the only TRUE leader, the Creator, the Ruler of all.

I vote for God!

I'm glad that's over. I revived as I walked back to my pew.

The piano began to play and the chorus of unique voices lifted praise to heaven.

My only hope was that I was a faithful servant of God's message. It wasn't about me; it was about God using me for His purpose.

OMG!

It's kind of fun to do the impossible.
—WALT DISNEY[25]

MY WIFE, MARY, ONCE ASKED me, "Why do you always find the most difficult thing to do and try to accomplish it?"

"It's not that I search for the most challenging thing to conquer," I said. "I don't mind the odds being stacked against me. I simply want to create something great. I like trying to improve upon something that needs help or establish something that has yet to be created."

It would be like taking over the coaching reins of a team that went winless the prior season, or building a team from scratch, or better yet inventing a sport that has never been conceived. Now that would be fun.

OneTen Management Group was that challenge. Also known as OMG, before OMG became the ubiquitous term used by the Gen Y generation, it was a company I started as a special event management and sponsorship sales firm. OneTen stood for the elusive 110% that was essential for absolute greatness. Of course there is no such thing as 110% because maximum effort would equate to only 100%. I used the term anyway.

OMG started in South Carolina and soon expanded with offices in North Carolina and California. We created new community music events in those states to improve the quality of life and attracted the required critical mass to further economic development in the cities we were hired to help. Revenue was good and cash flow was strong. After three solid years of building the business, I brought on an attorney as an equity partner to help with the legal element required with our plethora of contracts and negotiations. David was a solid attorney with the same ambitious vision of building something great right in his hometown.

We chose to change the course of the company by selling the event management divisions, which was the bulk of our revenue, and focus on developing a music and sports management company. It was something never before attempted in Greenville. It was either because it was too difficult or because no one else ever had the vision to give it a go. Nonetheless, we jumped off the mountain and built our wings on the way down. Our goal was simple: recruit and sign the best musical talent from the region, produce demo recordings, and negotiate record deals with the big boys in New York and Los Angeles. On the sports side, we would mine the talent-rich region and negotiate professional sports contracts in conjunction with endorsement deals.

The area had grown talent such as platinum recording artists Peabo Bryson, Aaron Tippin, and Edwin McCain, not to mention the mega-successful band Hootie & the Blowfish from just ninety miles down the road. As far as sports talent, it was equally abundant: Kevin Garnett, who signed the largest NBA contract in the history of professional basketball with a six-year $121 million dollar deal; Stephen Davis, a multi-million dollar NFL running back who honed his talent just twenty miles away; and professional PGA golfers Jay Haas and Lucas Glover, who were from our backyard. They were only the tip of the iceberg. The talent was plentiful and there was no end to the pipeline of future stars. It was a solid plan.

Nobody saw it coming.

No one would have thought our country would be attacked by Islamic extremists raining down a monsoon of terror with hijacked commercial airplanes. No one conceived our precious American way of life could change in a single day. No one thought our world would stop for a moment. It did. David and I watched the initial attack with a newly signed basketball player who we negotiated a contract for with the Harlem Globetrotters. The four-inch black and white television screen we watched the attack on didn't need to be a fifty-inch flat screen for us to grasp the enormity of the situation. It was going to affect potential investment dollars and the future of the company.

We were at a critical place in repositioning the company. Our efforts to raise financial support for the firm, as we strived to re-capitalize OMG, took a back seat to a global crisis. Our potential investors slowed their commitments as they tried to evaluate the financial effect that 9/11 would have on their own security and businesses.

Our bills didn't stop.

In the wake of 9/11, OMG became strapped with debt as we transitioned the company from the high-cash-flow event management business and redirected it with the new business plan. We took on bank debt, personal debt, and credit card debt as we lobbied potential investors. Timing was everything, and unfortunately our commitment to restructuring OMG was bad timing.

The investors came but usually with just enough money to pay for the next month's expenses or to get caught up on those stacking from the prior months. We never landed that one, big, difference-making investor to allow us to breathe and fully execute the ambitious but attainable business plan.

We persevered.

With the Boys Choir of Harlem as a marquee client on the sponsorship and music side of the business, we started signing local talent and vertically integrated the music division by acquiring the legendary Capricorn Recording Studio and other assets that would further allow us to reduce external expenses. Our music client base grew, with OMG artists from the Carolinas, Georgia, California, Ohio, and New York.

With our NFL and NBA agent certifications in place, we recruited athletes and set the stage for placing them at the highest level of professional sports. Despite the odds being stacked against us, David and I negotiated two fourth-round draft picks with the NFL Denver Broncos in our first year as certified sports agents. It was extraordinary, considering most certified NFL agents never even negotiate a pro contract and leave the business without tasting the fruits of representing a player in the league.

We were executing the plan and building revenue but not nearly fast enough to cover the overwhelming debt load OMG was carrying. David and I invested and loaned our personal savings to the company and opted out of our own salary for nearly a year at a time to keep OMG afloat. Our struggle to build the business didn't always go over well with our wives, but their support never fully waned. Our bills at home didn't stop either.

My father, who developed business projects around the world for fortune 500 companies, told me, "Gene, business plans usually take twice as long to accomplish as you originally plan and cost at least twice as much as you budget." He was right, as he always seemed to be.

David and I were in the trenches together, bailing water to keep the ship afloat while rubbing two sticks together trying to catch a spark and start a blaze of financial success for us and our investors. We supported each other but also fought like brothers. He had grown up in the South as a born-again Baptist, and I was from what most people considered the North and raised a Catholic. Once again, one of the closest people in my life was a born-again C-word.

His understanding of the Bible was solid, and he struggled along the road of his faith journey just like me and everyone else. We built OMG on integrity but fought to keep God first instead of putting success within the business as a first priority.

Through our collective faith journey, he helped me understand that being a Christian means you are going to make mistakes. That helped me realize that sins of the heart and sins of the flesh are the same in God's eyes; according to Jesus' words, hating someone in your heart was the same as murder. And as Jimmy Carter publicly stated, lusting for a woman in one's heart was the same as acting it out in the flesh. David helped me understand the concept of true grace as it applied to everyone, every day. He helped enrich my Christian knowledge and wisdom from countless hours together and marathon discussions about God, Jesus, and all things considered Christian.

We were Christians building a secular company that we tried to fit into our plan. We considered Christian music as a viable business group since we were cradled in the center of the modern-day Christian movement, but we passed, focusing instead on mainstream music with much bigger financial returns. It was a move that, if successful, would reward our investors with mammoth dividends.

Platinum-selling artist Edwin McCain came on board as an investor and then as a client by recording his next record at the newly remolded OMG (formerly Capricorn) Studios. We hired an accomplished producer from Los Angeles and relocated him and his family to Greenville. He had worked with super-star artists such as Matchbox Twenty and was a Grammy participant recipient for his contribution to the multi-platinum Matchbox Twenty *Mad*

Season album. The vertically integrated pieces were in place and OMG was poised for success.

We were scheduled to begin recording a heart-throb of a young man from Georgia who had the potential to be a prolific song-writer, a voice for pop radio, and a look that would make young ladies swoon and dig into their pocketbooks to buy his music, concert tickets, and merchandise. The table was set.

We knew we were on the cusp of massive success, a position that would peel the bankers off our backs so we could execute our business plan.

God had other plans.

The young singer-songwriter forgot his priorities and began missing gigs that we set up to help establish his fan base. His new-found girlfriend became priority one, which usually begins the writing on the wall and spells the beginning of the end. A new girlfriend at the beginning of a promising music career was usually not a good thing. After long and serious consideration, we had to determine whether or not to sink over $100,000 in the project or cut our losses.

One of our seasoned business partners made his feelings clear: "Gene, cut him loose and tell him to marry the girl." I did.

A hip-hop group we were in development with had been getting a lot of attention from the music industry. Lyrically the group was profound, mixing two edgy hip-hop and rap artists with a smooth R&B vocalist from Atlanta. As David and I sat in the office of the VP of radio promotion for Universal in Beverly Hills with the group's producer, we heard what we had been waiting for. After he scanned through the demo, he kept going back to the one song we felt could have huge radio success.

"Man, that song is a hit," he said as he cued it up to the beginning again. "I want to take this song and test it in a few markets, and let's see what happens."

We were on our way to breaking into the music game at the highest level, but there was a burning in the pit of my stomach. I had to state my peace with David about my internal dilemma.

"You know I love this record," I started. "But there is something that just isn't sitting right with me. You know I'm a big fan of rap, but I'm a bit unsettled about a few things."

David leaned back in the black leather chair and I leaned forward on the couch in the office lounge.

"This record hits you right in the face and pretty seriously with some highly vulgar lyrics only fifteen seconds into the intro on the record. I don't think we can release this album."

"Are you crazy?" David rebutted, raising his voice. "We put a lot of time and energy into this thing."

"I know. But think about it—our names will be on this CD cover as executive producers. That means we endorse it. Listen, I work a lot of hours away from my family working to produce a product, and I'm supposed to go home at night and not even let my wife and children hear the product I produce? That's crazy. I don't think we can do it."

God had reached into my gut and didn't let go. The journey for both me and David was always a struggle to keep our eyes on God's will as opposed to the veil of Satan's will. That battle was again waged for what Jesus would have done in the same situation.

David and I continued the discussion the next day.

"You know, Gene," David resolved. "You're right; we can't release this record."

A burden was lifted from our shoulders.

At the same time, God touched the life of one of the young rappers at a revival while the other slipped back into the streets. The R&B vocalist became such a financial drain, we had to let him go. We shelved the project while the band was self-dissolving.

In the period of mere months, our stable of national clients was reduced to an empty barn. Our cupboards were bare without an artist to produce and launch onto the national mainstream music scene.

God took away what we had been planning and working so hard to develop. But God wasn't done.

Within weeks, a young man visited our office brought to us by a former intern. Our producer listened to him in the studio and was overwhelmed with excitement.

"You wouldn't believe this guy I just met with," he brimmed with nervous enthusiasm. "He may be one of the most talented artists I have ever heard at this level."

"Great," I said with anticipation. "Where is he?"

"He just left."

"Let's get him back in here and have him play for the rest of us."

"Definitely, but there is only one thing."

"What's that?"

"He's a Christian artist."

Even though we were nestled in the Bible belt and making inroads into the music industry, we knew nothing about Christian music. It was an industry within itself. Different sets of executives, radio promoters, publicists, all of it. But it wasn't like we were overwhelmed with options, so we signed him.

I began asking questions and making calls, trying to learn the ropes of Christian music. I had never even been to a Christian concert before. Although we were theoretically starting from scratch, I at least knew the right questions to ask and who to ask. So many people, such as the executives from Brash Music, who also transitioned their record label from secular music to releasing an artist with massive Christian success, were forthcoming with helpful information and direction, something that was harder to come by in mainstream music. In mainstream music it was a dog-eat-dog world; conversely we found the Christian music circle to be a lend-a-helping-hand world.

We were Christians in the music business; we never had any intention of being Christians in the Christian music business. But we followed the path laid in front of us.

I attended my first Christian concert, Winter Jam. It was produced by the world's biggest and most successful name in Christian music touring and promotion, Premier Productions. If an artist could get aligned and booked on a Premier tour, their odds of making it would significantly increase.

I was shocked at the level of artistry, production, and quality of the acts. TobyMac was the headliner. The former member of the ground-breaking Christian group dc Talk was well on his way to topping his success with his former group. His performance and command from the stage was overpowering. I had never seen anything like it; had I not known he was a Christian act, I never would have known unless I really listened to his lyrics. My ignorance and miss-perception of Christian music was at an all-time high. My thumbs were sore from texting my family, friends, and business associates during the show. I wanted everyone to hear and see what I was witnessing. That concert changed the way I viewed Christian music, and that was a tall task for this music fanatic.

Our first Christian release was musically solid, but it received a chilly reception from the radio professionals. None of the Christian labels in Nashville expressed any interest in the project; few phone calls were returned. Despite the lack of interest, we, along with our business partners, negotiated a deal for distribution to all Family Christian Stores, the country's largest Christian retail chain with over 300 locations. It was happening one step at a time. If it didn't materialize through a traditional route, we took a machete and cut a new path.

As our transformation was in full swing, irony was at its thickest. As much as I tried to run from the Bible-thumping oppression of Jerry and "born-again" Christianity, our new artist wanted a special invitation to be printed in the liner notes of his CD, the first release on OMG Music. I cringed, but David and I agreed. On the inside of the CD booklet it read,

> Now What? If you're like I was a few months ago, and you think you're saved, but after reading this, you're not really sure you've truly accepted Jesus and His forgiveness into your life, THIS IS YOUR TIME!
>
> Here's how to accept God's free gift of forgiveness. It doesn't matter what you've done, how old you are, or what you look like. His gift is free, and all you have to do is accept it! I promise that Jesus will come into your heart and begin to change you into the person you've always wanted to be for Him. Just follow these steps to accept God's gift of eternal life and His forgiveness for your sins:
>
> (step one)
> Admit to God that you are a sinner and that you need His gift of forgiveness through Jesus Christ.
>
> (step two)
> Believe that God's Son, Jesus Christ, died on the cross and bore the penalty of your sins, and ask Him to come into your heart and change you.
>
> (step three)
> Confess Jesus Christ as Lord and Savior of your life, repent (turn away) from the evil things that you used to do, and commit to following Him.

Now just pray this simple prayer:
Dear Jesus, I admit that I'm a sinner, and I need your forgiveness. I believe that you died on the cross so my sins could be forgiven. Please come into my heart and change me for your glory. Forsaking my past sins, I will follow you as my Savior and Lord. Thank You for saving my soul and giving me eternal life. Amen

If you prayed this prayer, congratulations! You are now a child of God! You have been set free from sin![26]

The sinner's prayer! Are you kidding me? I thought to God. *Our first real record release and the sinner's prayer is printed in every CD booklet, and my name is in every one of those booklets as one of the executive producers . . . CLASSIC!*

It was a far cry from the profanity-laced hip-hop lyrics set for national radio airplay. I knew God was having a good laugh as He looked at me and revealed His plan for my life; He was taking me by surprise on a daily basis.

When I first proofread the booklet, I flashed back to the landing in Richland Hills. My faith had come so far, yet it brought me back to the place of origin: the sinner's prayer. But the words rang true! He was right; the words of the sinner's prayer were the essence of truth.

More unsuspected writing on the wall emerged. We had a number of the top management firms in Nashville agree to meet with us to consider signing our fledgling artist, a feat that took a considerable amount of phone calls and vigorous requests.

Then he called me.

"Gene, my father-in-law is going to manage my career," he said as I listened with utter astonishment. "God spoke to me yesterday and told me my father-in-law was going to be my manager."

Here we go again. I couldn't believe what I was hearing. I figured it was probably more like his father-in-law telling him he was the new manager. Nonetheless, who was I to say whether or not God had spoken to him?

The artist disregarded our business and marketing plan for his CD project. Instead of touring at domestic venues that would increase his fan base, as well as CD sales, he opted to focus on international mission work taking the gospel of Jesus Christ to all the nations. He was following his heart. How could I argue?

David and I still had a job to do; we needed a new project to generate revenue, one that would help fulfill the OMG business plan for our investors and bankers. With a new-found understanding and inroads into the Christian music business, we were open, we were ready.

But we needed to hold on. God was getting ready to step on the gas!

OMG
—The Second Verse

I like to listen.
I have learned a great deal from listening carefully.
Most people never listen.
—ERNEST HEMMINGWAY[27]

GOD'S VOICE WAS CRYSTAL CLEAR within the movement of OMG. He swept the deck of our secular musical artists and began to set the table with musicians and singers in an industry we knew nothing about. His voice was direct and without hesitation. He wanted us to apply our experience, skills, and gifts in the Christian music business. We listened and followed His lead.

: : : : : :

David and I were sitting with one of our new clients at the high-end steakhouse across the street from our office. The table was covered with white linen and carefully polished silverware. The future Jacksonville Jaguar of the NFL was enjoying his post contract–signing steak. Another NFL prospect—our business plan was working.

I excused myself without eating an entree to speed home and get ready for a dinner I didn't really want to go to with some neighbors. Although they lived merely two doors down, Lewis and Amy were acquaintances but not a couple Mary and I spent time with. I liked them, but they were not in our close group of friends. They went to the non-denominational, aspiring mega-church a few miles away while our family was safely nestled into our Presbyterian home. Our biblical views differed as well as our approaches to the gospel and its teachings; they were unabashedly on fire for Jesus Christ. We were on fire but usually contained our flames within a tight group.

On my way home I started to feel a bit under the weather. Beads of sweat formed on my face and a wave of nausea swept through my throat. Simultaneously, my stomach started to hurt, and I prayed I could maneuver the Range Rover to my house before I was forced to pull over and face the reality of my situation in a roadside ditch.

I barely made it to the house. I shouted to Mary from behind the bathroom door that I didn't think I could make it to dinner with Lewis and Amy.

"Come on, Gene," Mary snapped back with little empathy. "You'll be okay."

"I don't know," I appealed. "I really don't feel too good."

"You're fine."

It wasn't the support I was looking for, especially from my wife. I really didn't want to go, considering my circumstances. We had never gone to dinner with Lewis and Amy or on any other outing other than hanging out at a neighborhood function together.

"Where are we going?" I asked.

"Italian Market and Grille," Mary said.

"Italian Market? Why there? I don't even like that place."

"That's where they wanted to go."

It just kept getting better!

I tried to put an end to the madness, but Mary was having no part of it. I was feeling overwhelmed with an odd anxiety hovering over me. The nausea was an anomaly. I rarely felt nauseated and I hadn't vomited in over twenty-five years. The last time was my freshman year of college after the Drama Department party and an overload of grain alcohol-laced PJ and peanut butter cookies. I was well on my way back to my freshman year. But still there was no sympathy.

"Okay, here's the deal," I demanded. "Let me give them a call and tell them we will drive too so if we have to leave early it won't be such a scene."

Lewis was having no part of it.

"No, come on, Gene," he said. "Let me drive. I'd really like for you guys to ride with us."

He wanted us to ride together. It made absolutely no sense to me why we had to ride together. I had to make a course correction on my offer. I suggested that I drive. If I was driving I'd have more control of pulling the car over in case my nausea or lower intestinal struggle came to a head while on the highway.

"No."

They wanted us to ride with them in their family minivan. I wanted them to ride with us in my posh, shiny Range Rover. No luck. It was a mind-boggling struggle I had never encountered. At my suggestion to reschedule, my pleadings fell on deaf ears. No one seemed to care how I was feeling. My words were invisible.

For some reason I couldn't simply say, "No, we're not going," which wasn't a hard thing for me to say under any other circumstance. I didn't want to go, but they wouldn't relent. It was as if everyone was overlooking my infirmity of the moment, even my wife. I thought Rod Serling was going to stop the action any second and welcome everyone to the Twilight Zone.

Mary and I walked across our neighbor's yard to their house; I was hoping they would recognize my condition in the driveway.

"Gene, you don't look so good," one of them said.

Yes, I thought. *Now we're getting somewhere.* Perhaps this was the break I needed.

"Well, jump in the van, let's go."

I slid into the front passenger seat. Before I could get my seatbelt buckled, Lewis turned on the factory-installed radio.

"This is a band from our church," he smoothed. "Have you ever heard of them? Their name is Chasen."

"I knew it," I said to myself. It all made sense now. They had an ulterior motive for getting me to ride in their vehicle. They wanted the guy who was running a music company to hear a band from their church, a praise and worship band that led the music celebration on Sundays. He had played the whole thing beautifully. I was captive for the roughly twenty-minute ride to the restaurant. Just enough time to force-feed me with another aspiring band. Usually I had the option of listening to one of the hundreds of demo recordings stacked on my desk at my leisure. But Lewis was a cunning prospect and had planned the capture flawlessly.

The CD was cued up to the beginning, track one: "All Your Creation." The music began to blare through the speakers, swirling around my head like a cyclone. The electronic loop led to a clean acoustic guitar, transitioning into the electric six-string then a cacophony of loud noise. I didn't want to listen to anything. I simply wanted to chill as we drove down the highway and focus on steadying my uneasiness.

"Lewis," I warned. "Listen, I'm really not feeling the best, so just be ready if I need you to pull over. Seriously, I feel nauseous."

"No problem," he reassured me.

He leaned over and turned the music up.

I cracked the window open to get some cool air whisking across my face and hopefully to sweep some of the music away with it.

I didn't hear the music. I heard noise. It's not that the music was bad; at that point, Beethoven's Fifth Symphony would have concocted a clamor between my ears. I wanted to go home.

I was bound and forced to listen to a Christian band by a well-intentioned advocate for the Lord while a separate oppressive force pushed on me and kept me from hearing the essence of the band and its praising lyrics. A spiritual battle between good and evil was being fought around us in the minivan. If the music broke through to me, perhaps we would sign the band, record a hit song, have millions of people hear it on the radio, take the band to different towns and another country to perform while spreading the gospel of Jesus Christ, save the souls of some troubled kids who needed to hear Chasen's songs, get a record deal with a major label, make a name for ourselves, propel the band to success in the Christian music industry, and finally see our business plan fulfilled. That was a big *if*. But the music had to break through the barrier placed between it and my ears, my heart and more importantly my stomach.

Track two, "Our God and King."

"Well, what do you think?" Lewis asked.

"They're good," I stretched. "They sound good." I had to say something.

The twenty-minute ride felt like twenty hours. I needed the movement to stop. At the restaurant, I barely ate anything. I was just hoping we could get a little silence on the ride home. No such chance.

Track eight! "Waiting on a Disaster." It started with banging drums and driving guitar riffs. It was a disaster all right. I wanted my bed.

Then I heard the last line of the chorus, "God save the day."

God, please save the day, I thought.

Pulling up the concrete driveway, Lewis asked again, "Well, what do you think?"

"I liked it. I'd really like to listen to it more by myself if I could. Can you get me a copy?"

"Here, take this one."

"Thanks, Lewis. I appreciate it. I'll get it back to you."

"No, you go ahead and keep it. I'll get another one."

"Thanks again."

Shortly after I stepped in my front door, the overwhelming sensation waned. The heavy hand of whatever troubled me was gone. It was possible I could have caught the dreaded three-hour flu. It was also possible that Satan didn't want me to hear the music. It was quite possible that he knew if this band got a break they would save people for the glory of his adversary, for the glory of God. Satan could clearly see the future consequences of a lost battle. He tried, but God tried harder.

:::::::

On my own time, I listened to the music. It was all right for a self-produced recording. I had nothing to lose, so I called Chasen, the lead singer, weeks later to set up a meeting. They were scheduled to play as the opening act for Needtobreathe's first CD release concert, so our producer and I went to hear the band in person.

It was okay. He felt they had the basic essentials to make a very good record. "They sound like they could be the Christian version of the Goo Goo Dolls," he said. With him producing them, I felt it would be a great record.

We needed another willing band to sign. Christian or not, we needed a band.

Chasen became the band we gambled on for our next project and a shot at a major deal, something that was rare and unlikely for any new group. But Chasen had an exceptional quality; it was an innate talent to write prolific songs and touch the hearts of those in need of healing. The band had what was required to make a run at major Christian success.

The finished record was extraordinary. Our producer's mainstream talents helped craft the band's sound into a pop Christian group with enormous potential. But a CD is just a coaster in a plastic case unless it gets legs.

We sent it to all of the top labels and publishing firms for consideration with the hope that a major music company would pick it up and put their big music machine behind it. Record labels were inundated with so many demos and full-length CDs, it was difficult to rise above the clutter and get a music executive interested in a new project. New projects usually meant big investments. Having a radio-quality CD from a production company that was ready for distribution was an uncommon luxury for the major record labels. It meant they wouldn't have to advance any money for the production component of the new record. We felt ours was the one in a million to rise above the noise. It was one thing to send a new CD to a label rep; it was quite another thing to have them actually listen to it.

I followed up with phone calls to check where we were in the stack and to see if anyone had even listened to it yet, but returned calls were rare. I even met with some label reps and asked them to give it a listen with me in their office. That way I would be assured that they listened . . . à la Lewis and Amy. There was little to no interest; thus, no traction for a record deal, so the ball was still in our court. We made the strategic business decision to transition from a production company simply trying to produce records and up-sell them to the major labels to a record label ourselves . . . OMG Records.

We interviewed and hired the best independent radio promoter in the Christian music business. He had a long resume of success-ful #1 hit songs to his credit. He reminded me of Jerry Maguire in how he would work a roomful of radio program directors. He was masterful and relentless. We were disappointed that he refused to work with our first Christian artist, but he had made it clear that if the Chasen project presented itself, then he wanted to be first in line. He got the job. We hired a publicist, a booking agency, and a photographer. We set up our own publishing company to assist in the process of protecting the music. We invited in local radio personnel to see our studio and hear the music. I brought in Gary Gentry, one of the owners of Premier Productions, to also hear the music in the studio on proper speakers. If Gary liked it, then hopefully he would book our band for one of their tours. We, at the direction of God's hand, put a full-court press on the Christian music industry.

The radio promoter worked his magic at radio. After a few weeks, our first release, *Crazy Beautiful*, hit the radio charts. Week by week the song kept climbing toward our hopes then beyond our expectations. *Crazy Beautiful* finally stopped climbing, but not before it landed at #2 in the country! We had something special in our hands.

To further confirm our belief, the most renowned mainstream music promoter who worked with the likes of Madonna, U2, John Mayer, Alicia Keys, etc., called me out of the blue on a Sunday af-ternoon to tell me how much he loved the project. Jeff McClusky was *the* man in the mainstream music business. He listened to the CD with his daughter from his pile of thousands of demos after I had sent him an advance copy.

The calls didn't stop with Jeff. The phones were being dialed in the other direction. Nearly all of the big Christian music companies and some mainstream labels wanted to know about our new band. We had worked *Crazy Beautiful* to the top of the charts without any help from the majors. We were a small boutique label with no prior charting success. OMG Records was the only label on the Christian CHR charts without an affiliation with a major label. We had accomplished something extremely rare in any genre of music.

The time to audition for the Christian music industry in Nashville was ripe. We set up a showcase concert at a popular venue in the Music City. On the six-hour drive to Nashville, Jon, our in-house manager, called me to let me know the scheduled venue had been shut down and the doors padlocked! The concert was set to start in about seven hours, but we had no place to play and a full line of commitments from some of the presidents and other decision-makers at the major labels. Satan was working his heavy hand once again; or was it God?

We regrouped on the fly and Jon found another venue willing to host the show for $100. I feverishly called all of the commitments on our guest list driving through the Great Smokey Mountains and detailed the new plan. Jeff was even flying in from Chicago to see Chasen's one shot at wooing the industry.

The new venue was even better suited than the first. The sound technician was one of the best in the business, and he catered to our every need with his rough façade. Chasen and the rest of the band played the show of their life. They were poised to be the next big Christian band.

God had turned the potential train wreck into a smooth ride. He won yet another battle.

After nearly seven years of trying to sign a band to a major record deal, we were now in the driver's seat to negotiate the real thing.

With a pile of offers from record and publishing companies that wanted to sign the band, we made our strategy clear. Instead of a contract directly with the band, we wanted the deal to be with OMG Records. We were determined to be a major label imprint or at least the conduit for multiple projects. We had become a Christian music company and had a plan for a stream of artists we would produce and insert into the bigger music machine in Nashville on the OMG Records label.

In Lewis and Amy's minivan the music broke though to me, we signed the band, recorded a hit song, had millions of people hear it on the radio, and we took the band to different towns and overseas to perform while spreading the gospel of Jesus Christ. The music saved the souls of some troubled kids who needed to hear Chasen's songs, we got a record deal with a major label, made a name for ourselves, propelled the band to success in the Christian music industry, and finally we saw our business plan being fulfilled. Lewis and Amy's plan worked.

: : : : : :

Jon and I sat at the large conference room table surrounded by hip, black ergonomic chairs. People began to file in one-by-one wearing cool music industry clothes. I was overdressed in a fresh suit, a pressed shirt, and a stylish silk tie.

Everyone was introduced, then Jon and I were welcomed to the EMI family. We were now a part of the same family as Coldplay, Snoop Dogg and tobyMac. We had signed both distribution and separate publishing deals with EMI CMG, EMI's Christian Music Group.

The plan was being developed for our first major CD release, Chasen's *Shine Through the Stars*. I sat still as I watched and listened to how the machine operated. It was brilliant. It was overwhelming. It was perfect.

We made it, I thought with a smile. *This is it—we finally made it. We are in the elusive circle. We are inside the concrete walls of the music industry.*

I remembered the words of one of our music mogul mentors from New York who represented the Beatles, Woodstock, and Whitney Houston. He once told us in his Manhattan high-rise that one of the keys to making it in the music business is staying in business long enough for it to happen. He was right.

But, there was no time to rest. Our investors would be pleased at our success; however, there was still a long road to travel to financial profitability. It was time to get down to business.

: : : : : :

Lewis and Amy had planted the seed amid a firestorm of spiritual warfare. They fought for a young, unpolished praise and worship rock band from Powdersville, South Carolina. They stood strong and achieved what they were led to do.

God set our table with manna that He so generously provided. He convicted the hearts of two successful local business leaders, among countless others, to step up and invest in OMG when we needed it most to help the company continue. Through those two men, He taught us how to love and help when help is needed to fulfill His plan. God knew what He was doing. He knew the result of a victory in a minivan. He knew how to lead us from the padlocked venue to the perfect performance space. He knew what would happen if we succeeded with His business plan. He knew the trials and experiences we endured in mainstream business and secular music would lead to a new glorifying direction for OMG.

He knew that the ultimate success would not be measured on a balance sheet; it would be measured in the hearts and souls our Christian artists would touch.

In a flash, the new OMG was launched onto the Christian music scene. Only something drastic and out of our control could keep us from reaching the stars!

OMG
—The Last Song

Paul trusted God's plan for his well-being, he knew he had a future and a hope. Paul also knew that the reason most people never find that plan is because they are seeking to execute their own plan for their lives.

—RICHARD EARL SIMMONS III[28]

AT FIRST GLANCE, GOD HAS always had a funny way of revealing the Promised Land. Moses had been obedient to God and led the Israelites out of Egypt with the promise of a new home for his people, but Moses was never able to taste the earthly fruits of his labor for himself. God made His plan clear to Moses in the last chapter of Deuteronomy:

> Then Moses climbed Mount Nebo from the plains of Moab to the top of Pisgah, across from Jericho. There the LORD showed him the whole land—from Gilead to Dan, all of Naphtali, the territory of Ephraim and Manasseh, all the land of Judah as far as the Mediterranean Sea, the Negev and the whole region from the Valley of Jericho, the City of Palms, as far as Zoar. Then the LORD said to him, "This is the land I promised on oath to Abraham, Isaac and Jacob when I said, 'I will give it to your descendants.' I have let you see it with your eyes, but you will not cross over into it." And Moses the servant of the LORD died there in Moab. . . .[29]

OMG had turned the corner and was generating revenue from its various business groups: record label, publishing, touring, management, recording studio rental, and radio network. With all of the battles we had won and all of the obstacles we had overcome, we appeared to be headed for the Promised Land, the land of milk and honey. We could see it. We also saw how God was working within our lives, within the company, and within the lives of our clients.

Our redefined business plan was ambitious, but it projected realistic benchmarks. It was finally falling into place. It was taking longer than we had planned and it took more money than anticipated, but it was finally working. We could definitely see the Promised Land.

We knew the area was rich with oil. We had spent the prior decade on development and construction of our oil well, using our personal savings as well as the investment and loans of countless others. With the infrastructure and construction of the well complete, our first drilling hit the black gold, Texas tea, however slight the trickle. We simply needed a cash influx to operate the rig so we could fully realize the wealth of the region we successfully tapped.

David and I honed the business plan for one last offering from our investors. With the right clients signed, the record industry infrastructure in place, and revenue beginning to pick up, we calculated that we would need one additional cash infusion. The investment would allow us to manage the company debt load and operate the firm while investing in our current projects as well as future projects, ultimately placing OMG in a profitable position. After ten years of toil and reinvention, OMG was an overnight success story, depending on how success was calculated.

Writer Jill Devine once wrote, "Timing is everything—for this reason, patience is a vital ingredient in success planning. Patience will give you keys to the kingdom!"[30] She was right on many levels.

The *timing* of our final offering to our investors was *everything*. It was late summer 2008, the same time that the invisible ink began to appear on the wall. America was on the cusp of its worst economic meltdown since the Great Depression. Many of our investors and other potential supporters were successful businessmen and women with substantial real estate assets. Their concern wasn't whether or not they could afford to invest another $25,000 in OMG; it was how much of their wealth and fortune was going to evaporate from the virus that struck Wall Street. Their concern was their own family's security, not OMG and our recent success.

A few investors stepped up amid the national crisis and infused additional resources to protect their prior investment; but it was not nearly enough. David and I stood at the crossroads. One path was the Limp-Along Road, a path that may have ultimately led to a dead end. It still required financial resources, something I was able to take care of personally in the past. I had invested my personal savings, retirement, and children's college fund (my children's educational savings was something I promised myself I'd never touch). In total, I infused OMG with nearly $500,000 of my available resources, nearly everything I had saved. The other avenue at the fork in the road was Shut-It-Down Boulevard, a path I had never dreamed of looking down.

Entrepreneur and writer Bob Buford summed it up best: "Business, like life, is seasonal. Circumstances change." He continued. "Although I appreciate the wisdom in the old proverb that it's better to be lucky than smart, I believe that it's best of all to be bright enough to know when the party's over and when it's time to move on to the next event."[31]

David and I met with some key investors. We also met by ourselves. We consulted our wives in private. I sought advice from my father, my first and original investor. David and I prayed together.

Both paths looked dark and frightening. After extensive soul-searching and prayers to God filled with tears, we chose the latter: Shut-It-Down Boulevard.

We sold some assets and shut down the rest. After we officially made the decision to close OMG, my wife had her first restful night of sleep in months while mine increased with anxiety.

One of the things that disturbed me the most were the people at OMG that would be losing their jobs. I figured I would eventually be okay. Many of the younger employees would quickly rebound and find other jobs to sustain themselves and their families. The one person I feared for the most was Cheryl, our office manager and receptionist. She was ten years older than me and we had worked together for nearly fifteen years dating back to pre-OMG.

I originally hired Cheryl as a favor to a friend, her sister. Cheryl needed a job and she immediately pointed out to me that she couldn't type but she could answer the phone and file. I needed someone who could type but as a favor to a dear friend I hired her sister. I sent Cheryl to the local technical college to learn how to type and use a computer so she would at least have a marketable skill if she ever moved on to a different company.

Cheryl became one of the most dedicated and loyal employees an employer could ever hope for. She was punctual, always concerned about her quality of work, and she cared for everyone in the company as a mother hen would watch over her chicks. During one of our more troubling financial times, I asked her why she stuck around and didn't get another job.

"I want to see what's going to happen next around here," she said with a chuckle. "You never know who's going to walk through that front door."

Cheryl had seen a lot.

She not only saw my companies transform and grow, she saw how God transformed my life. When we first started working together, I was an agnostic at best, and she was one of those born-again Christians with extreme Christian and biblical views so contrary to mine. In the last few years of OMG, I came to understand that she was not only my employee, she was my guardian angel. God had placed her in that cloth chair by the front door to watch over me, to love and nurture me. She never judged, and she helped show me the way into the lap of God. She never hit me in the head with the Bible, but she was always ready if I had a question about the Word. She never condemned me or preached at me during our theological discussions; she always exemplified Christian love. Cheryl was my angel from God.

: : : : : :

How do you close down a company? I thought. There was a plethora of books and online resources detailing how to start a business and make it successful, but there was a lack of worthwhile material on how to shut a company down. The only real-life, practical option was talking personally to other business people who went through the same thing. For us, bankruptcy was not an option; the debt we carried could follow us for the rest of our lives, but we chose to deal with it face to face and not run from our obligations. Shut-It-Down Boulevard was treacherous like the Yellow Brick Road when things turned scary for Dorothy, Toto, and her three friends. Regardless of how depressing the reality of our situation was, there was always a beckoning light emerging from the Land of Oz . . . the light at the end of the path.

So many people had helped me and OMG survive through the years, I wanted to meet with as many as I could, one on one, to let them know what was on the horizon. Jack, a local successful businessman, looked at me over our table set with plates of "meat and three" and sweet tea.

"Gene, I certainly understand where you are, and I truly feel for you, but how do you do that?" he asked perplexed. "How do you go about shutting down a business? I can't imagine. I wouldn't even know where to start."

"Well, Jack," I responded. "This is it, this is where you start. I'm sitting here talking to you."

Jack had a string of high-end successful businesses and never had the privilege or misfortune of treading on a sheet of cracking ice that was certain to break through to the icy water below.

Although the water was freezing cold, I felt more like we were imprisoned in a furnace. My father, a retired GTE corporate business executive responsible for developing global projects, captured the difficult times in life through a poignant email to me:

> Just go about your business with honesty, integrity, dignity and humility. Above all, never lose faith in yourself. The tough times are life's way of building character. It's like fine steel . . . it needs to be subjected to intense heat and repeated pounding before it emerges as a superior product. And, while you're going through the tempering process take time each day to pray for guidance (your daily bread). While you might not get a letter of encouragement from Paul or a thunderous voice from the heavens, you will receive encouragement from surprising places, like a child.

He continued in a second email:

> . . . Not to mention the stress this put on your family life. How you managed to keep your professional team

together through all this plus lack of pay is beyond my ability to fully comprehend. The last two years would have crushed most men. You made it through it all, albeit with some business problems that will take just as long to remedy as they took to develop. . . . Most people believed in you during hard times. . . . The main thing is that you always believed in yourself. Mom and I did too. At times it was shaky belief but we buttressed it with prayers.

The love and encouragement my parents showed during stressful and dark times equally reflected the love and grace God has for me at all times.

A number of years earlier, when my children were much younger and OMG was going through one of its financial crises, it was apparent that Christmas wasn't going to be as bountiful under the tree as in prior years. At a time like that, it was nearly impossible to keep the reality of the situation away from the ears of my family. Mary and I discussed how we were going to tell our blonde-haired daughters that there were going to be fewer and less expensive gifts. The responsibility wasn't Mary's; as the financial provider, it was mine.

Caroline and Alexis sat on our floral-covered couch with their feet dangling above the carpet. I slowly leaned forward across from them on the brown leather ottoman.

"Girls," I said as I choked back a tsunami of tears with a lump in my throat. "There aren't going to be as many presents as last year. This year is a little different. We don't have as much money to buy gifts. Daddy is having a difficult time at work and there isn't a lot of money. But, we will all be together as a family and celebrate the true meaning of Christmas, the birth of Jesus."

Caroline, the older daughter, seemed to have a sense of acceptance and contentment about Christmas morning. Alexis looked oddly empathetic.

"Daddy," she said to try to soothe my obvious broken heart. "That's okay; Santa will bring us presents."

The dam of my eyes struggled to hold back my tears as the lump in my throat lurched. I felt I had failed my family; it was such a horrible sinking feeling. I could only think of one thing as I hugged my children for dear life. I cried to myself, *Alexis, I am Santa Claus.*

Sometime later I received a letter in the mail. There was an activity in church school for the younger children. The kids were directed to write a letter of encouragement to whomever they wanted by filling in the blanks:

> *To Daddy,*
> *Grace to you and peace from God our Father and the Lord Jesus Christ!*
> *Today in Sunday School at Fourth Presbyterian Church, we studied about how Paul wrote letters of encouragement to the churches he loved and couldn't visit often.*
> *I wanted to write a letter of encouragement to you because your company needs money.*
> *I wanted to tell you that ever thny will be ok. [I think she meant, everything will be ok.]*
> *I, Alexis, write this greeting with my own hand. The grace of our Lord Jesus Christ be with you.*
> *In God's Love,*
> *Alexis*

My dad was right. His email was prophetic: "While you might not get a letter of encouragement from Paul or a thunderous voice from the heavens, you will receive encouragement from surprising places, like a child."

Alexis was right. Everything would be okay. She didn't say it would be easy; she said it would be okay.

The dream of founding and running a business came true. The dream of representing a band and signing them to a major record deal came true. The dream of being a sports agent and representing a player in contract negotiations with an NFL team came true. The dreams turned to nightmares as the American economy crumbled with the help of greed and egocentric Wall Street bankers. OMG was pulled under by the force of the current.

We were not alone. Thousands of businesses closed across the country. Unemployment rose as America's workforce was laid off or welcomed by padlocked doors after their morning commute. Families broke up; sane, well-respected individuals walked into banks with guns, like Clyde Barrow attempting to steal some cash, to provide for their families. Others slipped into depression; some committed murder, taking the lives of coworkers or bosses, while others turned the gun on themselves in an attempt to escape from the reality of 2008.

But others turned to God. They sought refuge in His love and grace. They turned to Him for guidance and encouragement while they stood in the unemployment line in the hopes for a weekly handout to put food on the table while they diligently looked for work. Others, whose businesses still had life, turned to Him in the hope He would reveal the way to turn their businesses around and create even more jobs. Turning to God in the hardship was a way to escape the peril.

For me, God was the only true way to escape it. He used OMG to prepare me for the next stage of my life. He tempered my resolve. He taught me lessons, honed my skills, and changed my heart. He was training me for what He had planned next. I was clearly a student of His plan and not the commander of my own. I just had no idea what the plan was or where His plan would lead me. I was a husband and a father without a job. My financial resources were limited, but they would afford me *some* time to search for where He had hidden the map for my future.

One thing was for certain: I would be spending more time at home with my family while dealing with the fallout from OMG. I would be busy, but I had time to rest.

Alexis was right: *everything would be okay.*

Where I'm Supposed to Be

*O most holy Christ, draw me, weak as I am, after Thyself, for if Thou
dost not draw us we cannot follow Thee. Strengthen my spirit, that
it may be willing. If the flesh is weak, let Thy grace precede us; come
between and follow, for without Thee we cannot go for Thy sake to cruel
death. Give me a fearless heart, a right faith, a firm hope, a perfect love,
that for Thy sake I may lay down my life with patience and joy. Amen.*

—JOHN HUS[32]

THE LINE TRAILED OUT THE double glass doors and turned
down the sidewalk to the end of the building. Most of the people
standing in line looked relatively ungroomed, wearing old clothes,
while some of them emitted a weathered, unbathed stench. A few
of the patient people who waited in the queue were well dressed
but wore a long, sad face.

The unemployment line is a humbling row sprinkled with people
from all walks of life. Most of my circle of friends and business associates, including me, never imagined we would be standing in the
line of government assistance. I once thought it was simply a place for
losers looking for a handout, but with the ever-present reality of the
American economy, I realized it was a place to help pay for rent and
put food on the table. It was a temporary hand *up*, not a handout.

I hoped to keep from tapping into my retirement, so any additional qualifying funds was a blessing to help support my family. I
stood there with joyful humility and a thankful heart. I didn't look

at it as demeaning or embarrassing; I looked at it as an experience I thought I would never have and I was grateful for it.

I was blessed with a time of rest but certainly not relaxation. I aggressively prayed and asked God what He wanted me to do. What should I do with the rest of my life? How could I best serve Him with my talents and skills? I wanted to be helping in places devoid of hope so I could use my gifts to offer hope.

I set my personal parameters for my next career: I wanted to be in non-profit work. I was tired of running the for-profit rat race and felt I was best suited to use my skills in a non-profit capacity. I knew my calling was to serve our world and minister to those hurting and in chaos. My materialistic desires to stack a vault full of cash were replaced with a longing to serve others. Second, I wanted to be in a faith-based environment. My new-found Christianity drove my desire to be in a work community filled with love and a mission to glorify His name. And thirdly, but not necessarily that important, if there was an opportunity to do non-profit Christian work associated with music, it would simply be a plus.

The one organization I knew of that fit all three parameters was Premier, the world's largest and most successful Christian music promotion company. I called on one of the founders, Gary, de-scribed the situation at OMG, and let him know that I was available if anything opened up at one of his companies. Although the bulk of the Premier companies were for-profit, I knew they had started a foundation twelve years earlier to bless others with their success. Working for the Premier Foundation would have been the perfect job that fit within all three parameters. The only problem was there was no job at the Premier Foundation; the board of directors ran it without any employees. Nonetheless, it would have been the perfect place to work.

I made a long and detailed spreadsheet of job opportunities with the Premier Foundation at the top. I had three options for my search: One, apply in the non-profit world in both Christian and secular organizations. Two, apply in the mainstream workforce in sales or management. Three, consider starting my own company again, a non-profit ministry or a traditional business. God had been good to me and I wanted to honor Him by aggressively searching for employment in all three areas.

It was also time to learn. I hit the bookshelf and began to read the books I had neglected for so many years. God's call was still not clear, and there was a constant tugging to learn more about the church. I attended a lay school for theology in case God paved a path for the pulpit. Despite the whispers that I was attending the seminary, I simply took a class on Church history, a detailed journey from Jesus Christ to today's Church universal. The one thing that stood out from the class was that man has tried to re-invent Christianity with each decade. Man has glossed over the truth of Christ's life to make it suit personal desires. I concluded that Christians were the primary enemy to Christianity.

I took interest in the lives of the Gofourthers, the elderly and retired members of our church ranging in age from 65 to 95. I spent time on group outings, afternoon bingo, and one-on-one visits with my gray-haired brothers and sisters. I learned that they are the most important resource and gift in our church, in any church. They are rich with history, knowledge, and wisdom. I was ashamed I hadn't spent more time with them before.

I organized a number of church mission trips, including one for ten people to Belize during the Thanksgiving holiday. But as God touched the winds, an enormous storm covering the entire Gulf of Mexico, Hurricane Ike, smashed ashore near Galveston, Texas, claiming life and causing utter destruction. Mary suggested we change our focus from Belize to those hurting on the Gulf Coast. We did. Instead of working in a coastal country in Central America, our families slept on a church floor in Beaumont, Texas, and helped offer peace to Mrs. Taylor, who had never spent Thanksgiving away from her house in Texas until that year.

During a brief work break, I, along with a few of the middle school and high school kids, walked into the adjacent graveyard. Refrigerated semi-trailers lined the old, historic African American cemetery. The trailers served as the temporary resting place for the coffins that popped up out of the ground during the storm. The area we were working in was at sea level; thus, the coffins had no place to go but up when the water began to rise.

Vaults and coffins littered the solemn lawn as we walked through and read the headstones. One coffin we saw was made of wood. It had rotted since the 1970s and was cracked in two. We peered inside the crack and saw the lady inside dressed in a pick dress and wearing her string of pearls. The sadness of Ike's aftermath even transcended beyond the living.

On Thanksgiving Day, after eating with our host church, our group drove to Crystal Beach, just north of Galveston. I had seen a lot of destruction and sadness in my day, but Crystal Beach was different. It was a vast and eerie wasteland. It looked as if God had taken His hand and wiped the slate clean. Almost nothing was left. When we closed our eyes and listened, it sounded, felt, and smelled like a serene beach paradise. With eyes opened, it looked like a post-apocalyptic landscape with nothing more than cement foundations and broken wood columns. A dozen cars were buried half-way deep in the sand. We were the only ones on the deserted island.

It was a vivid reminder that what man creates is temporary: the beach houses, the restaurants, the telephone poles, the cars. It had been changed. It was equally as poignant that what God created never changed: the waves still rolled up on the beach as they did before the storm. God's creation was permanent; man's creation was fleeting. I was helping plant seeds of hope and wisdom in the hearts of my fellow missionaries.

I saw the difference the trips to Texas and Alabama made in the lives and hearts of those participating. I wanted to be in those disaster-stricken areas. My heart cried and I wanted to help. I wanted more people to see the destruction, and I prayed God would change their hearts to act too.

In an effort to continue to move forward with all employment options, I formed a board of directors for a new ministry. The board members were businessmen that had all been on a mission trip with me before. I knew they "got it." I wrote a business plan and crafted a budget. The purpose of Hope Disaster Relief was to *inspire hope by our deeds.*

The mission of Hope Disaster Relief was developed to be implemented with Christlike love. The core mission was found in three fundamental initiatives:

1) To restore and maintain hope in the hearts of those affected by disasters.

2) To repair the disaster-stricken structures where people live and worship.

3) To develop teams of volunteers who are willing to work and inspire through the principles of faith, hope, and love; in turn, the volunteers are blessed with a renewed spirit, commitment to service and are enriched by the act of inspiring hope out of chaos. The mission's first priority is focused on those survivors in the United States.[33]

Even though Hope Disaster Relief was a viable option, I felt God still wanted me to put a full-court press on other job openings while I was developing HDR. My family and I met and we were willing to move to New York City or Chapel Hill, North Carolina. My search focused on non-profits and ministries in those cities as well as locations within a 100-mile radius of Greenville. I would consistently find myself narrowed down to the final two or three candidates for management, development, and fundraiser job openings. But the job offers never came. I was either overqualified or the organization felt I was too much of a gamble for a charity to hire someone from an entrepreneurial background.

: : : : : :

I waited in the exquisitely appointed lounge of the Franklin Hotel on Franklin Street in Chapel Hill. It was icy cold outside but it felt right. The University of North Carolina campus was a beautiful colonial setting and would be perfect for my new home. I had been narrowed down to the final four for a development job in the UNC School of Law. In addition to my resume, excellent interviews, and being a Carolina alumnus, a friend and classmate from my days in the Journalism School was hiring for the position. I knew it was a slam dunk! I wanted that job! It was my plan!

The Law School had brought me in a few weeks earlier for a tour and personal interviews with the search committee as well as with the dean. The interviews couldn't have gone any better. Finally, I felt I was in the perfect position to be offered the job.

He and I ordered a drink and settled in on the couch and leather armchair next to the crackling fire. We started with small talk. I knew. I could tell.

"Gene, we've offered someone else the job," he said with disappointment. "There was an internal candidate that was qualified and already knew the system. I'm sorry."

"It's fine," I said with melancholy relief. "I figured I was a long shot anyway."

"Well, actually, it was a very hard decision. It was between you and this person and it almost went your way. Your qualifications are extraordinary and the interviews went great. The dean even said that he was wondering why he had to interview someone with your background, but after the interview he knew why. It was extremely tempting to hire you with your contacts and experience. You would have done well in the position."

I was relieved. God made the right decision. If I had been offered the job and taken the position, the job would have required extensive night and weekend hours. Since Caroline would be a senior in high school, my family would have stayed in Greenville for one year and I would have had to rent an apartment in Chapel Hill during the week. The reality of the job would have separated me from Mary and the girls and could have pulled my family apart. Getting turned down for something I really wanted was the best thing that ever happened during my job search.

It appeared that God still wasn't clear as to where He wanted me. Or I just had not recognized it yet. Or He just had not revealed it yet. It wasn't time.

: : : : : :

My job search took me down roads and into places I had never imagined. I was turning over every reasonable rock looking for the answer to my future. If a lead looked like God had placed it in my path, I followed it.

The 750-foot mountain looked more like a hill. The trees on Mount Luke were bare, and the cold air in Little Rock, Arkansas, created a pristine setting. My goal was to hike to the top and converse with God. I called Mary back in South Carolina in case my heart didn't make it to the top or I wandered from the trail and got lost before dusk set; she would at least know where to tell the authorities I was last heard from.

Little Rock was the location for the discernment retreat for the National Response Team of Presbyterian Disaster Assistance. My new-found passion for disaster relief work led me to be one of ten people considered to serve as a volunteer for the Presbyterian Church USA in disaster-stricken areas. I was all-in when it came to helping others in hopeless circumstances. The National Response Team was early on the scene of natural and man-made disasters in an effort to determine how our denomination would be best suited in long-term recovery. I welcomed it as an honor and a privilege to even be considered as part of the sixty-five-member national team. Ultimately, I was invited to be a part of the team. It was a serious responsibility as I committed to represent the Church and volunteer in places suffering from a disaster.

Mount Luke was a challenge. I was in okay shape but not nearly as good as I should have been for an aggressive hike. I was search-ing for my place in God's plan and I needed some time alone with Him. I put my iPod on and scrolled to the Old Testament in my playlist. I seemed to learn more from the spoken word than the written text.

Although the climb seemed short, it was a lot more arduous than met the eye. The trails were faintly marked as I climbed and meandered up the mountain. King David spoke through my iPod when I neared the apex of Luke. As I approached the top, I gasped for breath and broke out in a slight sweat amid the chilly air.

The view was clear. The surrounding splendor was just as it was meant to be. I could see for miles as the two resident bald eagles circled above. I looked down at the open stone chapel and the placid lake next to the lodge. I toggled to Jeff Buckley's version of "Hallelujah." The normal daily static between God and man seemed to dissipate. I was still. The song played and my emotions swelled as I cried out at the top of my lungs.

"What do you want from me?" I yelled. "What do you want me to do?"

I started to feel anger and frustration as my cries seemed to go unanswered. I wanted an answer!

The wind briefly swept across the top of Luke. One eagle perched while the other kept circling. I pressed pause on my black iPod.

"Okay, You got me here, now what? Now show me where You want me to be!" I demanded.

Silence.

Was God answering or was He ignoring me? I couldn't tell. I sat on the bench that had been built for reflection as it was positioned over the camp.

Wanting an answer to my future, I closed my eyes and tried one more time, "Where do you want me?"

I opened my eyes. He answered me. It wasn't a booming voice, nor was it a vision on the lake. The answer was as clear as it was before I demanded an answer.

God wanted me where I stood. He wanted me on the top of Mount Luke in Little Rock, Arkansas. He wanted me to see His splendor. He wanted me to be in the midst of other Christians discerning our place in His Kingdom.

At that moment I knew I was exactly where He wanted me to be.

The Second Half

*God's desire is for you to serve him just by being who you are,
by using what he gave you to work with.
. . . But in the final analysis you alone must choose how you want to
live. You have the freedom to decide whether or not you want the rest of
your years to be the best of your years.*

—BOB BUFORD[34]

FINANCES WERE DWINDLING BEYOND MY comfort zone. It
took me a while to overcome my angst on the monthly bill payment
day. I had to reprogram myself to thank God for providing us with
the resources to write the checks for the bills instead of being pan-
icked about tapping into our retirement. It took a couple of months
but I was finally able to write the checks with a grateful heart.

I hadn't worn out my welcome at home; however, Mary was ready
for me to be gainfully employed once again. I needed to get a job!

Being president of a privately held company that closed wasn't
exactly a shining endorsement on my resume; even though OMG
in many ways was a success story, it was still one of thousands of
companies that shut its doors amid the financial meltdown of 2008.
Fortunately many business divisions of OMG lived on under new
ownership, such as the radio network and recording studio, while
our music artists found refuge with new labels. The company I
started, and that David and I built, was still living on.

My entrepreneurial career had tremendous highlights, including business successes and numerous awards for leadership, communication, fundraising, and creativity. However, I ended up on the losing side of the coin for various positions I was perfectly qualified for. Rejection could be motivating; it could also be downright depressing.

My attitude, in the face of pressure, was almost always upbeat and positive. I had a close circle of supportive friends, including the seekers in our Wednesday morning Bible study I started with some close friends. I wanted to be a leader and an example to others while facing an uncertain future, even to the guys I leaned on for support.

I contended that my situation was the best thing that ever happened to me in my professional career. I had a time to rest, a time to reflect, a time to chart a new course for the rest of my life. But there was one thing abundantly clear: I needed to get a job.

While conducting humbling face-to-face meetings with my Christian music business partners in Nashville, a close friend invited me to save a few dollars and stay with him and his family in Franklin. Marty was in a similar situation, searching for his next life after Christian music publishing. He was always recommending interesting books for me to read.

"Gene, I've got a book that would be perfect for you," he said with assurance. "It's called *Halftime*. It's about the two halves of our lives. The first half is usually focused on success and climbing the corporate ladder. The second half is about living a life of significance based on what you learned in the first half."

"That's perfect," I said.

"Here, take my copy."

Marty was right. The book was exactly what I needed to read. I gobbled up Bob Buford's *Halftime* like a pocketful of jellybeans. I was living it. My life was smack dab in the middle of half time.

I had time to reflect and plan, just like during the half time of a football game. While sitting in the locker room after the first half, I looked at my life. I analyzed what I did right and what I did wrong, what worked and what didn't. It was a time for rest, reflection, and planning. When the second half was ready for kickoff, it would be full of adjustments based on what was learned in the first half. The second half was where the game was won or lost. It was time to win the game.

Buford eloquently described his journey as if it were my own:

> For me the transition into the afternoon of life was a time for reordering my time and my treasure, for reconfiguring my values and my vision of what life could be.

> *That's exactly where I am,* I thought. *I needed to reconfigure my life goals!* It represented more than a renewal; it was a new beginning. It was more than a reality check; it was a fresh and leisurely look into the holiest chamber of my own heart, affording me, at last, an opportunity to respond to my soul's deepest longings.[35]

Halftime reassured me that I was right where I was supposed to be. Most of the other guys in the Wednesday morning Bible study were approaching middle age and had lived a life of success through business. Some of the others were also desperately in need of a job. It was the perfect book to introduce as a study tool to aid in figuring out the eternal question, "Why are we here?" It was also good to answer the question, "What are we going to do with what we learned so far, and how are we going to use ourselves to glorify God?"

: : : : : :

Gary and I continued to talk by phone and meet occasionally for lunch. I had hoped he would just say, "Hey, Gene. Welcome aboard the Premier train. We have the perfect job for you." That wasn't the case.

As he paused from his chef salad covered in Thousand Island dressing, he said, "I'd like for you and your wife to come on our next cruise, the Music Boat."

I was familiar with that division of Premier, Premier Christian Cruises, and the work they did. I had plenty of time to scour their website before our meetings. Premier Christian Cruises would charter an entire ship from Royal Caribbean or Carnival then reprogram all of the onboard entertainment with Christian music's top bands and artists, faithful speakers, authors, comedians, and other outstanding family activities. The two-thousand-plus guests on the ship were all surrounded by the best entertainers and other Christian passengers. The casinos and bars would still be open during the cruise but were usually relatively empty. The ship was full of Christians who weren't oddly looked at because they were reading a Bible next to the pool. It was a dream vacation for anyone either searching for God's truth or comfortably walking hand-in-hand with the Father.

"Gary, wow!" I said with shock. "I'd love to, but we can't afford that right now."

"You two would be my guests. You'll just have to get to the port in Florida and we will take care of the rest."

"I don't know what to say."

"Say yes," he returned with a Grinch-like smile.

"I can't speak for Mary, but we'd love to. Thank you so much. Believe me, this comes as something both of us could definitely use right now."

It was the first time Mary and I had ever been on a cruise. There is something special about cruising, especially the first voyage. The experience far surpassed all of our expectations. The cruise filled my heart and confirmed that Premier was a special company. They produced Christian events that glorified God for the nearly one million people who attended their concerts, conferences, camps, and cruises each year. It was a major company with a small working staff. Premier had a specific mission to spread the gospel of Jesus Christ through its events. I wanted to be a part of their team.

Gary introduced me to Roy, one of the other founders, as we sat by the café's glass window overlooking the Caribbean and the passing waves from the ship's bow.

Gary and Roy were at the fork in the road. As board members of the Premier Foundation, they needed to decide whether or not to liquidate the assets of the foundation and donate them to other Christian charities or take a leap of faith and hire someone to run the organization. Timing was everything; I was out of a job and they were considering hiring. If they chose to shut it down, my search would turn to putting all of my efforts into Hope Disaster Relief since the job offers weren't pouring in. If they opted to hire a new president for the foundation, I hoped my name would be at or near the top of the list.

Knowing that I had committed to a self-imposed deadline of the first week in June to move ahead with HDR, as I discussed with my board, or accept a job that could provide for my family, I popped the question.

"Do you know when you will be making a final decision on your intentions for the foundation?" I pressed.

"That's a good question," Roy followed. "We need to make up our minds soon."

"I have another option I have committed to follow through on if this doesn't work out. But quite frankly, working with Premier is and has been my first choice all along."

"How much time do you have before you make your decision?"

"I've got about ten days."

"Okay. We'll let you know in ten days."

The rest of the cruise was filled with unparalleled anticipation. There was hope, a chance. I knew in my heart it was a long shot, but there was still a chance.

I stopped by one of the ship's bars on my way to our cabin to tell Mary about the meeting. I sat alone on an ordinarily packed row of stools. The bartender was a nice-looking, dark-haired man in his thirties wearing a white jacket. His name tag read, *Singh, India.* He told me how much he enjoyed the Christian cruises because it gave him time to rest from his mixology and it offered him a reprieve from drunken passengers.

Our conversation quickly turned to religion, as I was curious about what he believed and why. Most people's religion is based on their geography, where they were born, and what their parents believed. Singh was no different. As I answered questions about the Christian faith, I explained the differences between Catholics and Protestants. Singh looked at me with a perplexed brow.

"Protestants are Christians?" he asked.

I kept in my chuckles. "Of course."

"I always thought that Protestants didn't believe in God," he followed.

From a bird's-eye view his line of thinking made sense. Protestants . . . protest. Protestants protest against religion. I could see his perspective. Fortunately I was fresh from my theological training on the history of the Church. I detailed the break from Catholicism and its efforts to get back to the true teachings of Jesus Christ.

He was curious about the Bible, so I found an extra copy on the ship we had brought with us and cheerfully gave it to him.

Sometimes, I thought, *the best place to break down Christian barriers and share the true meaning of God's love is the place you least expect.*

MercyMe and tobyMac headlined concerts that lifted every hand on the ship to the sky in praise for the Great Provider. Tears were shed in humility and thanksgiving for God's loving grace. We were a speck on the ocean sailing with a solitary mission: to glorify God.

:::::::

Purgatory.

I waited. I held my breath for ten days. Waiting.

I kept the ringer on my Blackberry on loud at all times, not knowing when the call would come. There was no way I was going to miss Gary's call, if he called. *What is going to be God's call?* I thought. *Running a disaster relief ministry or heading the non-profit arm of the world's largest and most successful Christian music promotion company?*

I waited.

I was secure with either role, but I had an unrelenting desire to work in an established Christian ministry. Premier was perfect. I saw how the leaders of Premier operated their businesses, always doing what was right even if it didn't directly benefit them financially. They were respected businessmen who loved God and even ran their for-profit businesses like dedicated ministries.

I waited.

With every passing day, I clutched my cell phone anticipating the inevitable "Gene, we're just not ready to make a decision about the foundation." Or "Gene, we think the best thing at this point is to close down the foundation and liquidate its assets." Or "We've decided to go in another direction and hire someone else for the job."

I waited.

The eighth day . . . no call. The ninth day . . . no call.

On the ninth day, our Wednesday morning study group finished our journey through *Halftime*. It was the second time I had read the book, and the witching hour had come for me to set my course for the second half of my life. I was ready for the rest of my years to be the best of my years.

I waited.

Day ten. The final day. Mary and the girls were home and roaming around through the house as I tried to remain composed in our guest room turned office. My entire family was well aware of my nine-month search for peace, the quest for my next big responsibility and provision for my family. I told my girls that it was a big day: I would either be full force with Hope Disaster Relief or taking hold of the reigns of a position that had to be created within the Premier Foundation. It was *the* day.

My Blackberry rang at full volume. The name on the screen read *Gary, Premier*. My heart was electrified like being hit with a defibrillator: full voltage. My palms moistened. It rang for a second time; I didn't want to appear too anxious. I waited. I pressed the green button.

"Hello," I calmly answered, contrary to my anticipation, as if I didn't know who was on the other end of the call. "This is Gene."

"Gene, Gary," my speaker sounded. "How's it going?"

"Great. How's it going with you?" mustering every ounce of control.

"Good," he said. I knew Gary wasn't much for dragging out important conversations. "We want to offer you the job to run the foundation."

I was beyond shock! I couldn't believe what I had just heard. His words formed complete sentences but my mind could barely compute the meaning. The job I wanted from the very beginning, the first call I made in my job search produced fruit. Not only was it a dream job, I couldn't imagine a better place to serve God. He knew exactly where I needed to be, but He also knew I needed more time, about nine months, to mature into the position He graciously created. For once, the call I wanted for my life was actually the same as God's call for my life.

"Thank you," I said as I composed my thoughts. "Let me talk it over with Mary and I'll give you a call back tomorrow."

"Sounds great. I look forward to it."

"Me too. Gary, again, I really appreciate the offer." I pushed the red button on the Blackberry.

A sense of relief engulfed me as I sat in silence. My heart was happy.

"Well?" I heard as Mary's voice traveled up the stairs. "What did he say?"

I was still without words.

"Well? Was that Gary? What did he say?" her voice got louder.

"He offered me the job," as I held back the tears of sheer elation and humility. It was Christmas in June. I simply couldn't believe it was true.

The job wouldn't be easy. The foundation needed to be reorganized with a refined mission and a solid plan for raising money and granting its resources to worthwhile and qualified Christian charities. The opportunity came with a blank sheet of paper and the task of figuring out how to fill it up, how to proceed. I accepted the position with open arms and a full heart.

Gary knew my commitment to the Presbyterian Disaster Assistance National Response Team and the fact that I could be called away at any moment to serve those affected by an immediate disaster. He was also well aware that I led mission trips throughout the year and I was called to continue organizing and serving on those trips. Those were responsibilities I felt I couldn't compromise.

His response was clear and direct. "Gene, I think that's great. It's a wonderful example to others of you living out your faith."

I told my daughters that when I started looking for a job I set simple parameters: as a first choice I wanted to work in non-profit, I wanted the non-profit to be in Christian ministry, and if it dealt with music that would be a bonus. And strangely enough, the job I was offered didn't even exist when I charted my course. It was clearly the will of God that the job was created and offered to me.

It took a while for my disbelief to wear off. As I opened my eyes the next morning, lying next to Mary, I asked her if the call from the day before was just a dream.

She laughed. "No, it wasn't a dream."

: : : : : :

As the evaluation and reorganization of the foundation neared completion, the plan for the new Premier Foundation began to take shape. I knew I was in a special place working with special people, but the reality of Premier's truth wasn't completely apparent until I received a forwarded email from one of the concertgoers at one of Premier Productions' Winter Jam events. After I read it, I knew why Premier existed:

PRAISE REPORT

Hi Steve, I am Whitney and I am 18 years old. I have had a terrible past involving multiple rapes, drug use, and witchcraft, not Wicca, but witchcraft, like Satanism. I at-tended winter jam last night and I got saved. I am now free from my sin, free from pain, and do you know? I had been planning to kill myself at 3:33 this morning? Thanks to Jesus, the radio station, and whoever else made Winter Jam happen, I am ALIVE :)

You'll be hearing from me again because I want to volunteer or donate or something, I just wanted to let you know what God did for me last night, Keep me in your prayers because it is already hard not to fall back on my very recent beliefs. God Bless, Whitney.

It was clear. Premier existed for God. Plain. Simple. We were a weapon in Christ's war on evil.

: : : : : :

In a working community of faith, it's often difficult to understand why other people don't worship God and thank Him for every blessing He bestows upon us. In the tight circle of the Jesus cult, we frequently look from the inside out and wonder why others don't see what we do, not understanding why they don't fully accept that Jesus is the Son of our Creator. God is clear, He is intentional, and He is always there providing the answers to our heart's questions. Some people don't know how to see the answers, others are kept from the view by their own barriers, and still others choose not to look at all. Sometimes there is serenity in the dark, but it never lasts. Fear always creeps in when our hearts realize the serenity is merely a façade. Only the light reveals and cleanses the evil that lurks in the dark.

In a working community of faith, there is love. There are business meetings that begin and end with prayer. There are conference calls to simply connect with people's lives and to lift up prayers for each other as we navigate each day. There is a keen focus on the least of us who desperately need a helping hand. There is a call to a greater purpose than just getting paid and making money. There is a social and divine responsibility to our neighbors, wherever they reside. In a working community of fathomless faith, there is unfiltered love.

I was finally in a job I would never have conceived while pedaling my Schwinn in Richland Hills, or running wild at UNC, or meandering through an agnostic funk. For all of my life I had envisioned living in the biggest house in town with global success and egocentric notoriety, sitting on a stack of cash. For much of my life, I unsuccessfully tried to run from the Christians; but they found me at every turn. When God removed the scales from my eyes, I finally saw that I wasn't running from the Christians, I was running to them. In fact, I had become one of them.

I was finally home.

The True Face of Katrina

I can change the world
With my own two hands
Make a better place
With my own two hands
Make a kinder place
With my own two hands I can make peace on earth
With my own two hands
And I can clean up the earth

And I can reach out to you
With my own two hands
—BEN HARPER[36]

GOD MOVED ME LIKE A chess piece during my last months at OMG and throughout job search. I was ultimately placed firmly on the black square on the board that read *Premier*. He was also using me in a simultaneous chess match in New Orleans. I traveled back and forth to Louisiana leading groups to serve the survivors of Hurricane Katrina. Each trip revealed a higher level of consciousness for everyone who took part. My gifts were being used to help bring my fellow volunteers closer to God.

: : : : : :

Red *x*'s marked the dilapidated row of houses. The weathered spray-paint still stood as a bold reminder that nothing had been done to the houses in ages. In each quadrant of the *x* were either numbers or letters signifying who checked the house, when they searched the building, and the number of dead animals or humans found inside. Nearly four years after Hurricanes Katrina and Rita ravaged New Orleans, causing more than $81 billion in damage, the remnants of their destruction were as vivid as if they had happened the day before.[37]

The stark scene saddened my heart. It also saddened my daughter Alexis's heart, who was fortunate to witness the decay by my side. I couldn't fathom that the state of reconstruction of one of America's greatest cities was a stalled decrepit mess. New Orleans lost over forty-three thousand rental units, and over five thousand apartments were bulldozed. Some of the city was back to life as it was before the storms. The French Quarter was vibrant; of course, that area was the primary lure for tourist dollars and television cameras. Most of the stately homes and nice white neighborhoods were back to life, having been rebuilt with insurance money, FEMA cash, and other means of restoration.

But the heart and soul of New Orleans, the neighborhoods where the people lived that made the city great, were still drowning in the flood waters of negligence, misappropriation, corruption, and sheer denial. The government and most Americans had turned their backs on the Crescent City, choosing to move on to the next shocking disaster. Americans wanted to get on with their own lives. But New Orleans still needed help.

There was a wave of national help from cities and communities all across America reaching out to offer food, shelter, and a new way of life for the hurricane's survivors. Many Gulf Coast residents were bused to towns all across the map without their consent. A handful were sent to Greenville, South Carolina, and housed in the convention center until their future cleared.

Greenville's convention center was less than a mile from the Range Rover dealership that supplied my transportation. I dropped my Rover off for service one afternoon and when I came to pick it back up, it was nowhere to be found. It had vanished. A few months later, the midnight blue Range Rover was found in the disaster-stricken region of Mississippi. It only made sense that if someone was going to steal a vehicle to get back to their bayou home, it should be a new Range Rover fresh from an oil change with a full tank of gas.

: : : : : :

On my first disaster recovery trip to New Orleans, God blessed me by putting many resilient residents in my path. Two men in particular, living galaxies apart but separated by mere miles, taught me how to care and gave me reasons to love.

Ernie was a frail, gray-haired, retired marine who had been living in a FEMA trailer for nearly four years after Hurricanes Katrina and Rita. He spoke with a gruff attitude laced with sincere appreciation for our time and assistance in rebuilding his home. His single-story, white brick ranch home was accented with light blue shutters and trim. The formerly all-white neighborhood had been repopulated with African Americans over the years. Ernie seemed to resent the fact that he was the only white resident left on his street, but he wasn't overtly racist, only occasionally. It was not my place to judge; it was only my place to love.

His once-white aluminum FEMA trailer was weathered and fit for demolition. It was a crime that a retired veteran and loyal resident of New Orleans had to endure four years in a space barely big enough to serve as a storage shed. His wife refused to sleep in the trailer so she moved in with her sister across town. I didn't completely understand why she didn't stay with her husband until he invited me inside his temporary home one day. It was a wreck.

Ernie, a lifelong resident of New Orleans, had to be hooked up to oxygen twenty-four hours a day because of his lung condition. The clear tubing wrapped around his head and fit loosely under his nose where the pure oxygen filled his lungs. He was a broken man, living in a broken trailer, next to his broken house. There was no acceptable reason why the renovations to his house weren't completed.

Ernie and I grew to be close friends. Every time I brought a new mission group down to New Orleans, he would insist I bring them to his home to meet him, the American treasure I called E.J., or Mr. E.J. to the youth. I'm not sure if he needed me or I needed him or we needed each other. I heard his stories over and over and grew closer to him with every visit. He just needed someone to listen. I saw him as family.

On my second trip, Don, who had jumped in feet-first with an enormous heart for missions, Ross, and I noticed the condition of Ernie's old Saturn sedan. He had been riding on his spare tire and the other three were as bald as Kojak. Without hesitation, we told him we were taking his car to get a tune-up and four new tires. "No questions asked, no debate, that's that!" I told him.

After delivering the car to Pep Boys, I got a frantic call on my cell from E.J. "Gene," he raced with his raspy voice, "Have you dropped the car off yet?"

"Yeah, why?" I answered.

"I left my loaded pistol tucked between the seats covered by a yellow towel."

"Well, E.J., it's a little too late now. It should be fine, but when I go back to pick it up, if the parking lot has a few police cars in it, there might be an issue," I laughed.

Sure enough, when I picked it up, there was the gun underneath a towel, right next to a rotting, moldy peach.

When the Saturn was returned to his home, Ernie, the hardened marine, quietly wept with humble appreciation, and my heart blossomed because I knew it had been the right thing to do. On his first drive after the new tires, he called me from his cell phone.

"Gene," he yelled. "It's E.J. My baby's running like a Cadillac. It rides like it's brand new. Thank you, thank you so much. I can't tell you how much it means to me. I love you guys, I really love you guys."

After nearly five years of living in the eroding tin can in his front yard, Ernie finally moved into his renovated home. He was sleeping on the sofa in the living room because he couldn't get the rancid mattress out of the FEMA trailer. He said he was going to pull it in the house and sleep on it on the living room floor.

No way, I thought.

The next trip down, we hauled a brand new mattress and box spring to Ernie's home. Once the furniture store owner knew what I was up to, he sold it to me for next to nothing. It was a perfect accompaniment to the new bedroom suit someone else had donated to him.

These weren't acts of kindness we just wanted to do; Christ required us to do them. We were loving our neighbor as God loved us, even if the neighbor was ten hours down the highway. Although we are taught not to proclaim our good deeds, the most important piece of our kindness is that it was done in front of our youth in many instances. They saw our selfless efforts while asking nothing in return. They saw the mustard seeds we were planting, and our hope was that they too, one day, would perch on the branches and scatter seeds of their own.

Even though Ernie had moved into his renovated home, he was relatively alone. Reverend Charles Duplessis, on the other hand, was living in a brand new house built by the Mennonite Church and was constantly surrounded by family and friends.

Reverend Duplessis had no choice whether to renovate his home or not. He lived only two blocks from where a levee breached. The 200-mile-per-hour wall of water that hit his home completely destroyed his wood-frame structure on Tennessee Street as well as demolished his church and community center on Flood Street. If the force of the rushing wave hadn't ruined everything within his house, the 20-foot-deep standing lake of water in the Lower Ninth Ward completed the job. The Ingram Barge Company vessel that broke through the levee was resting only a stone's throw away from where the Reverend's house once stood.

I had seen Reverend Duplessis on television on the Larry King Show and heard about his relationship with Brad Pitt. Brad and Angelina had started the Make It Right Foundation in the Lower Ninth Ward to give back and help rebuild the blighted area. Brad had adopted New Orleans as his second home and wanted the Reverend to be a part of the Pitts' rebuilding project because the minister was the iconic rock in the Lower Ninth. However, the Mennonites from Illinois stepped up first and agreed to rebuild the pastor's home in record time.

I walked up the wooden steps to his front porch and was greeted by a towering, noble man with a face that could have served as the template for Mount Rushmore. Reverend Duplessis always stood with his head high, as a man with conviction and dignity. He commanded respect by his bearded presence but stood with resounding humility and unwavering love for the Lord and those around him.

The Reverend was a Vietnam veteran and lived in his home with his wife, Thirawer, of nearly forty years. They nurtured three daughters plus two adopted children and countless others who crossed the threshold into their warmth. He and his wife subscribed to the old proverb, "It takes a village to raise a child."

Reverend Duplessis wrote about his home:

> Our house was like *the* house of the neighborhood; it was called "The Kool Aid House." Even before we did the pre-Katrina renovation on our house, people would flock to our house and we just couldn't understand it. Why would they come in? We had something to offer, ourselves. And if you offer yourself, somebody's going to come.

He continued,

> God has sustained us by faith. We're rebuilding the house and trying to rebuild the church. If it wasn't for the churches, I know we wouldn't be where we are and so many other people we've talked to say the same thing.[38]

Even though his home was rebuilt, he was still strapped with the mortgage on the house that was carried away with the storm. He accepted the fact that he still had monthly payments on something that didn't exist anymore. He never shirked his earthly responsibility.

The Reverend extended his hand and swallowed mine with his rock-solid but gentle shake. It was followed by a warm hug. It was a handshake that memory never forgets. His deep and commanding voice was what you would expect God to sound like; Morgan Freeman had nothing on the Reverend. He was the model of determination, resiliency, leadership, and love. Other than my father, he was the most impressive man I have ever met.

He told us of his horrific journey from New Orleans to Alabama during the pre-hurricane evacuation. He expected to be away from his home for merely three days but wasn't let back into the Lower Ninth Ward for almost three months. Hurricane Katrina hit, then Hurricane Rita made landfall less than a month afterward. Government officials opted to re-flood the Lower Ninth Ward to mitigate damage to the main part of the city, the tourist destinations. His home, or what was left of it, stood under twenty feet of water once again. On the third anniversary of Hurricane Katrina, only 19 percent of the population had returned to the Lower Ninth Ward.[39]

But there was not a hint of bitterness in his voice while he told his stories, including those of blatant racism toward him and his thirty-seven traveling companions. He calmly described the inept government response to the needs of his community and the overwhelming red tape strapping the impoverished residents. He was a man without resentment, and he was in touch with God's will for his life.

With every mission trip to New Orleans, no matter the size of our group, Reverend and Mrs. Duplessis always welcomed us into their home for fried catfish dinners, fellowship, and worship, while never asking for anything in return. There were always grandchildren running around, family members and friends dropping in, and an uncanny love for all men. He was the closest thing to true Christian love that I had ever encountered.

In an effort to top our Thanksgiving mission trip to Beaumont, Texas, a year earlier, I planned a trip for New Orleans that included sleeping on another church floor for our all-white fourteen-person team. The Duplessis family hosted our group plus countless others in the community for the Thanksgiving dinner of a lifetime.

Although it was business as usual on Thanksgiving Day on Tennessee Street, it was a feast Emeril himself would have bowed to, including baked catfish, crawfish dressing, greens, macaroni and cheese, gumbo, and turducken. The conversation from the kitchen composed a joyous melody blending with the clanging dishes, pots, and pans. The laughter seeping in the door from children and adults playing football in the backyard while the announcers broadcasted the Detroit Lions on the television was the perfect symphony. Thanksgiving at the Duplessis home was a feast for all the senses and was how it should be celebrated: a multicultural celebration of love, giving thanks and praise for God's countless blessings.

As with Ernie, I had requested that friends consider helping support the Reverend and the rebuilding of his Mount Nebo Baptist Church and community center. My friends always responded. I spearheaded the campaigns without being asked from the Reverend. I always felt led to serve him and Ernie.

As a graduate of New Orleans Theological Seminary, Reverend Duplessis understood he didn't need a fancy church building to hold worship services to glorify God. His three-hour Sunday services, as well as the special Wednesday worship gatherings he held for the mission teams, were staged in his dining room and living room with folding metal chairs. The congregation would wander in at any time during the 180 minutes. A small boom-box provided the music while everyone in the house offered their voices to God. Words for the hymns were projected on the wall, sometimes. The Bible verses weren't predetermined. They were selected as the Reverend opened the Bible. He once asked one of my daughters to read a Bible verse before his sermon.

"Which one?" she diligently asked.

"Any one," he said with his enormous smile. "Whichever one you want. You pick it."

She read a random verse suggested by her older sister, then the Reverend delivered a riveting forty-five-minute sermon as if he had planned that verse all along. He had no notes, no script, just the Word of God in his heart and an unparalleled knowledge of the Bible.

When he really got going he hopped and stomped a bit. I noticed he had kicked his boots off and was making his moves with his gold-toed socks. I couldn't help but laugh at the beautiful scene I was participating in; it was spectacular. As a Catholic turned Presbyterian, I had never enjoyed church as much as I did when I worshiped with Reverend Charles Duplessis in his living room in the Lower Ninth Ward.

He, like Ernie, I considered family, a brother I would lay down my life for because I knew he would do the same for me. There were thousands of Ernies and Reverend Duplessises in New Orleans. I was unable to help all of them, but I was able to help one at a time and at the same time help myself.

The words of Reverend Charles Duplessis continued to resonate with me: "If you can come, you need to come and see." There was no way to adequately describe the situation in New Orleans without seeing it firsthand.

In the course of one year, I had taken five mission trips to New Orleans, leading nearly seventy people to the city on the Mississippi River. With every trip, eyes were opened to the horror of Katrina and Rita's aftermath and hearts were transformed to pick up the torch of love and care for our fellow man. God had used me and my gifts for His glory. He had me where He wanted me. I was executing His plan on the uncomfortable and unsuspecting, mean streets of New Orleans, 600 miles from my cozy pillow-top mattress.

: : : : : :

Megan sat at the end of the median on Poland Avenue. Her tanned California face was pale and covered with the film of the street. The Ninth Ward lived hard, almost an indescribable existence until you have had the privilege of walking the buckled concrete pavement in person.

Megan's blonde hair was tinted brown from time, a long road, and pain. Her partial dreadlocks draped around her shoulder. Her clothes were dirty, very dirty. She didn't smile. Megan gazed down Poland Avenue in the direction of the Mississippi River. She appeared void of emotion, blank, empty, tired, sad. Megan was beautiful.

Two days earlier while leaving the work site on the way to lunch, I first saw Megan. She was on a different street corner but holding the same sign: "Everyone needs a little help sometime." I could not move my eyes from her face. She stared straight ahead like a zombie in a trance. Her daze affixed me.

Normally I would have rolled down the tinted window of my SUV and helped the stranger . . . the beggar. This time I didn't. I was the deer and she was the headlight; I couldn't move. I wanted to know. I wanted to know why, how, when, who are you? God sighed for Megan. I cried for Megan.

I wanted to talk to her. The street light clicked from red to green. We rolled. The questions came with me and the answers were still sitting on a stone curb underneath tattered threads on the street called New Orleans.

I wanted to turn around, park, and ask her the questions that tormented me. But I didn't. I drove back to the work site. Although Megan and I were a million miles apart, she was with me in my heart. She was with me before I ever saw her, she was with me where I stood, and she would be with me the next day.

Megan's situation haunted me. Her soul was bearing down on me. Her face was under my eyes; her dirty face was accented by a silver loop nose ring in her right nostril.

I asked her in my mind, "Where did you sleep last night? Where did God's child sleep? Were you safe? Did you eat? Where are your parents? Where are you?"

The work team finished an epicurean's dream. We ate at the world-famous *The Joint* BBQ restaurant. Full and content, our group of volunteers had money, we had means, and we had opportunity. We drove to the Duplessis home on Tennessee Street to drop off an almost-new bicycle for their granddaughter that Alexis wanted to donate. The day was bright and clear but a crisp 60 degrees for the Big Easy.

We crossed the Industrial Canal from the Lower Ninth Ward and turned right onto Poland Avenue as we talked and kidded each other. My throat tightened and all frivolity left me. I saw her again, for a second time. She was on a different street than the first time I saw her. That girl, there she was. This time, time was with me. As the cars in front of me passed through the light, I slow-rolled and waited until I was right next to her. Red light.

I was the staggered deer again. I quickly told the story to my coworkers as precious seconds ticked away. I didn't know what to do. I wanted to take the day to talk to her. I wanted her story. "I don't know what to do," I uttered out loud.

A fellow mission volunteer in the back seat blurted, "Give her some money."

I didn't want to contribute to a bad habit; I wanted to solve her problem. I needed to talk to her because I couldn't solve her problem until I identified her problem and its cause. I really didn't know for sure what ailed her.

I pressed the button and the window dropped into the door.

"How old are you?" I shot.

"Nineteen," she muttered as she tilted her head toward me.

"What's your name?"

"Megan," she said as she gazed at me through the slits of her eyelids.

Her beauty continued to strike my heart. The beauty of God's child was embodied as a talking statue on a dusty curb.

"Where are you from?" I pressed.

"California."

"How did you get here? How did you get to where you are in life?" I continued. I begged for an answer I could accept. I prayed for an answer to satisfy my soul.

"My boyfriend told me he had a place for me to stay so I came out here and then he couldn't make the rent." She answered my question but it left me hanging.

"Do you do drugs?" I pressed. "Don't lie."

"I smoke a little weed," she spoke in her depressed monotone.

"Well, here's a few dollars. I'll pray for you and I love you. God bless you."

"Thanks."

The street light clicked green. I pushed the button and the tint reappeared from the door, creating a barrier between Megan and me. We rolled.

My throat tightened again as I had to keep the tears from breaching the levee. I whispered to the other guys in the Chevy Suburban, "My daughter Caroline is eighteen."

To the passing tourist or volunteer worker, Megan was the face of New Orleans. She was the face of New York, Los Angeles, Chicago, Birmingham, and Nashville. Megan was the face of every wayward youth in every city and town looking for a way out, a way up. Unfortunately, she had no idea where she was going or what she was doing. She was just trying to survive the night.

It was my responsibility to let her know that I loved her, the same as God loved all of His children.

New Orleans was the tip of the spear, ground zero for the battle between good and evil, separating heaven and hell with a pencil-thin line. It was a classroom for anyone willing to learn and the testing platform to find out who we really are as children of God. The Crescent City represented despair and hope, caring and indifference. It was a city filled with our brothers and sisters in need of Christian love.

New Orleans was the place to stare Katrina in the face and ask God, "How can I serve You? How can I help?"

The Fruit

. . . Being a Christian, or follower of Jesus Christ, requires much more than just having a personal and transforming relationship with God. It also entails a public and transforming relationship with the world. If your personal faith in Christ has no positive outward expression, then your faith—and mine—has a hole in it.

—RICHARD STEARNS[40]

I HAVE ALWAYS WANTED TO make a difference for the greater good of our world. Even during my agnostic malaise, there had been a deep burning to leave a permanent mark that proved I was here, signifying that I did make a difference for good.

Too often we look so far outwardly toward a global perspective that our own local community is disregarded and replaced by the suffering child in Africa. Even more important still is the example we set within our own family and the positive mark we leave on our own children.

In September 1967, a television public service announcement first aired that drove the message home. It showed a three-year-old boy hanging out with his father, doing things that fathers and sons do. Every time the dad did something, the boy followed suit and imitated his father to the tee. It starts out with the announcer saying, "Like father like son." Dad paints the house, the son paints the house. Dad drives the car and gives an arm signal as the directional; the son rides in his car seat with a play steering wheel and gives an arm directional signal as well. Dad washes the car, the son washes the car. Dad picks up a rock and throws it, the son does the same. Finally, the loving and caring father picks up a pack of cigarettes and fires up the tasty cancer stick. His precious three-year-old boy picks up the pack and looks inside. The announcer's voice comes back on and says, "Like father, like son . . . think about it."[41]

It's a poignant statement that we should imitate the actions of our Father, but it is also a stark reminder of our responsibility to our own children. Young children like to imitate their parents. In most cases, they want to be just like Mom and Dad. Our children are a significant representation of who we are; thus, we should always have a keen understanding that our actions plant seeds in the hearts of our children and those seeds will either produce good fruit or bad fruit. The same holds true for our friends and those closely connected to us in our daily walk.

In Matthew, Jesus eloquently describes the result of being a nurturing example:

> ". . . Every good tree bears good fruit, but a bad tree bears bad fruit. A good tree cannot bear bad fruit, and a bad tree cannot bear good fruit. Every tree that does not bear good fruit is cut down and thrown into the fire. Thus, by their fruit you will recognize them."[42]

In the Book of John, Jesus is quoted in even greater detail about the importance of learning and teaching, while clearly stating our responsibility to love:

> "I am the true vine, and my Father is the gardener. He cuts off every branch in me that bears no fruit, while every branch that does bear fruit he prunes so that it will be even more fruitful. You are already clean because of the word I have spoken to you. Remain in me, as I also

remain in you. No branch can bear fruit by itself; it must remain in the vine. Neither can you bear fruit unless you remain in me.

"I am the vine; you are the branches. If you remain in me and I in you, you will bear much fruit; apart from me you can do nothing. If you do not remain in me, you are like a branch that is thrown away and withers; such branches are picked up, thrown into the fire and burned. If you remain in me and my words remain in you, ask whatever you wish, and it will be done for you. This is to my Father's glory, that you bear much fruit, showing yourselves to be my disciples.

"As the Father has loved me, so have I loved you. Now remain in my love. If you keep my commands, you will remain in my love, just as I have kept my Father's commands and remain in his love. I have told you this so that my joy may be in you and that your joy may be complete. My command is this: Love each other as I have loved you. Greater love has no one than this: to lay down one's life for one's friends. You are my friends if you do what I command. I no longer call you servants, because a servant does not know his master's business. Instead, I have called you friends, for everything that I learned from my Father I have made known to you. You did not choose me, but I chose you and appointed you so that you might go and bear fruit—fruit that will last—and so that whatever you ask in my name the Father will give you. This is my command: Love each other."[43]

The lasting effect of who we are can clearly be seen in those who are the closest to us. Although we may not think we see the fruit of our labor, it's poignantly evident around us and in the hearts of our children. God blessed me with the gift of grace and salvation that I rudely rejected. He was persistent and I eventually accepted the gift, and it has grown within me. But I wasn't sure how it would affect my family; more importantly, my children have even greater power than I do to leave a lasting and powerful mark on our world.

On a daily basis, I could see traits and characteristics in my children that I exhibited regularly. Some of them were positive and heartwarming while others caused me to pause and say to myself, *Wow, that's me. I wish she didn't pick that up from me. I didn't know she was listening or watching.* One thing was abundantly obvious: my children were *always* watching and *always* listening to their father!

Raising Caroline and Alexis in a loving church was the best thing Mary and I ever decided to do. So, in the church is where I saw the real fruit of my life blossom within my children. I knew I was at least doing something right.

At fourteen years old, my youngest daughter, Alexis, gave the message to an elderly group of people at a Presbyterian retirement home. I was joyfully shocked at her Christian insight and understanding. She read aloud:

> "Therefore go and make disciples of all the nations." That is a very high demand for eleven people to take on. However, those eleven disciples did a wonderful job of spreading the word and love of the Lord Jesus Christ. I have been made a disciple through many different experiences. I was practically born in the church. I was baptized, went to little kids Sunday school, then later Cross-Way Jr. Highs where I had many enriching experiences, I became commissioned into an official member of the church, now I'm in Sr. Highs and I almost always attend big church. I even

go to a Christian school. Despite all of these experiences, the one that has called me to be a disciple of Jesus the most is mission trips.

This past June, my dad who is 45, Joe Brown who is 75, and myself who is 14 decided we would go down to New Orleans on a mission trip. This was one of the best decisions we could have made. I was not sure at first if I really wanted to go. About 80 other people were staying in this church that has been converted to a house for missionaries. Neither my sister nor my mom was going and I really did not want to stay in a room with a bunch of other girls I did not know. I debated not going but in the end I felt that God wanted me to go. So I packed my things and we got in the car for a ten hour drive down to Louisiana. When we got there I still was not very positive if I was going to like this or not, I would soon realize that I would like it very much.

Our small group of three got paired with another group of three from Wisconsin. We worked on a man's house for the next five days. His name was Mr. E.J. He was a former marine and a very tough guy. He had been living in a trailer outside of his house for the past four years. He has just recently moved into his new home. Our group grouted the bathroom floor, the kitchen floor, laid down ceramic tile, put up cabinets and a few shelves. In the short amount of time, we had accomplished a great deal. Not only was there the satisfaction of completing physical things, but there was the satisfaction of starting something spiritual in myself, our group, and Mr. E.J. God called the six of us to be a disciple and spread the love of Jesus through mission work. When we worked on his house, we took breaks and he would come out and tell us stories; some about the hurricane, others about his family, and some about his friends. He had a kind of passion in the stories that he told that I began to admire. He understood what God had provided for him and he was very grateful for all of the work that we put into completing his home. We spread God's love through physical labor and he expressed God's love through the stories he told.

Each group was assigned a project leader. I did not know it at the time, but now I am almost certain that God handpicked ours. His name was Tim. Although he did not spend a great deal of time with us during our working hours, the experience outside of that time changed my life forever. His wife took groups just like ours to see the Ninth Ward and other very destructive parts of New Orleans. The wreckage was beyond anything fathomable. We drove through this one street that looked just like any other. She said, "We are going to go to Reverend Duplessis's home. He and his wife have an incredible story to tell." She laughed and said, "I don't have a hard time getting people to go in, I have a hard time getting them to leave." I thought okay I'm sure he is not THAT great. He actually was.

Our group of six and Tim's wife stepped inside this man's home. From that moment on, I was never the same. When I meet a new adult I put on a very happy smile and a totally cheery attitude. I realized that the Reverend matched my smile and my attitude but with a greater joy. His story was so inspiring because of the struggles he had to go through. It made me feel bad for ever complaining about my life when his was so hard. After his story was done we stayed for another hour and just talked to him and his wife. I knew they were disciples. Every movement they made was through the love of Jesus and for Jesus. They believed so strongly in him that it was as if they were one of the disciples on the mountain with Jesus. I had never met a stronger Christian before. When I left I realized I was not putting on a smile or a happy attitude anymore, it was permanent.

I now know that the task Jesus asked the disciples to undertake was not impossible. If all of them were like Reverend Duplessis and his wife then spreading discipleship to all the nations was not a chore, but a joyous task. I am happy to say that June 2009 forever changed me into the disciple that I am today. Because of this trip, I am able to go and make disciples of all the nations.

It blew me away. She was so young but she still got it! On that day, God, as well as Mary and I, smiled.

Alexis continued to represent an awe-inspiring growth from the experiences I afforded her. She had a heart for helping others and wanted to do something about it. After the *Greenville News* caught wind of her new project, they decided to feature her in the newspaper. Columnist Jeanne Brooks wrote:

The idea came to her while sitting on porch steps in New Orleans. Alexis Krcelic, now 14, and her father were with a church group helping repair a house damaged by Hurricane Katrina. That day, they were grouting floors.

She'd taken a break. While sitting outside, "It popped into my head that I wanted to open a cooking school for kids," she recalls. Caught up by the idea, Alexis went directly into the house and told her dad, Gene.

"He laughed a little bit and said, 'OK.' Because I have a lot of ideas and projects I come up with."

But she kept thinking about it. She decided she wanted her cooking school to be nonprofit and to reach underprivileged children. "There are already cooking schools for kids who can pay," she explains.

Classes at her school might one day lead to careers as chefs. But mainly Alexis was interested in teaching kids how to cook and eat healthy for not much money, so they didn't feel they had to rely on fast food.

They would learn about good nutrition. And the kitchen skills that kids picked up at her school would serve them well a lifetime—for both their health and their budgets.

Even after returning home to Easley, Alexis kept thinking about her idea. She came up with a name for the school: Cook It Forward. Still the problem was, "I didn't know where to get the money to get started. I'm a 14-year-old girl."

Then her dad one day read about Pepsi Refresh Project (www.refresheverything.com). The company was holding a nationwide online competition for grants to good causes. Each month, the public would vote online for 1,000 new ideas, and the top 10 vote-getters in each category would win grants.

Each month up to $1.3 million in all would be awarded. And the top 100 runner-ups in each category would automatically be entered in the next month's contest for another chance.

. . . After high school, Alexis wants to take a year off and do mission work in Africa. Then she hopes to go to Columbia or Harvard University and major in business so one day she can open a bakery in New York City.

It would be the kind of bakery that people stop by after dinner out in a restaurant or when they're just walking along the street.

With any luck and enough votes, Cook It Forward will be well established by then.[44]

Alexis didn't win the grant, but her initiative and desire to help others was profoundly obvious. By being exposed to the needs of others, she picked up the torch to help light the way for others.

:::::::

High school students are often faced with endless struggles, exciting challenges, and difficult decisions, none more so than which college to attend. College charts the course for the rest of a young person's life.

Having been raised a rabid UNC fan, my oldest daughter, Caroline, had Chapel Hill on the brain and at the top of her wish list. She had a clear vision of what her plan looked like and where it was heading. I knew it would be difficult for her to get accepted to UNC from out of state, but she had excellent grades and Mary and I were alumni. She had a shot at *her* plan.

At Fourth Presbyterian Church, the graduating high school seniors lead worship during the annual Youth Sunday celebration with each senior giving a quasi-sermon and a time of reflection. It was still another chance to see if anything Mary and I did or said as a parent took hold within Caroline's heart.

She stepped up to the pulpit with incredible poise and spoke with a non-wavering voice. She was in command. Caroline looked out over the congregation and said:

Today is youth Sunday . . . and Mother's Day. We honor our mothers who brought us into this world and have helped nurture us. And in two weeks, it will be Reverend McSween's final sermon at 4th as our senior pastor. A man who has also helped nurture us. For our mother's and Dr. McSween, we are deeply grateful.

On January 22, 1992 I was born in Greenville, South Carolina. I was named after the place where my parents met, Carolina, the North Carolina Tar Heels that is. I have grown up loving baby blue and everything North Carolina, and disliking everything Duke. I knew when I went off to college I would become a Tar Heel. As I got older, that dream became less of a reality due to the incredibly high admission standards for out of state students at UNC; such as high SAT scores, class rank, academic standing, extracurricular activities, and the fact that I live in South Carolina. When I got denied from North Carolina this January, I was pretty upset. But I knew my backup was Clemson University (anyone can get into Clemson . . . right?), and I now had my heart set on becoming a Tiger. Clemson is about 30 minutes away; I have good grades (over a 4.0 average), ok SAT scores, and plenty of extracurricular activities. Well on February 12th, I got a small envelope from Clemson. I opened it and it said I was accepted to the Bridge Program at Clemson for entrance in Fall of 2011. This is where I would go to Tri County Tech for a year and then transfer to Clemson. After I read the letter, I went upstairs to my room and cried, and cried, and cried!

I asked God why he didn't let me get into Clemson? Why was I not good enough?

My parents tried to cheer me up, but no luck. Even though I knew what they were saying was probably right about how everything would work out for the best, I didn't want to listen.

Then I found a way to appeal the decision. I wrote a letter to the Admissions Board stating why I should become a Tiger, and I got numerous letters of recommendation from some of you as well as distinguished alumni.

I received another letter in the mail about a month later saying they were sticking with their decision about sending me to Bridge. I was devastated. I didn't feel that I was good enough and almost every day I would come home from school and just want to cry because I was not going to the college I wanted; the college of my choice. My plan! I asked God why this was happening. Why could he not just follow MY plan?

I wasn't excited about college anymore because none of the remaining schools were really a part of my plan. After a few days of considering College of Charleston, USC, and a significant offer from Presbyterian College . . . I decided I was going to attend the University of South Carolina. I was going to become a Gamecock. I was less than thrilled about this decision, but I felt it was the best option for me. I was still heartbroken over being rejected by my two dream schools, you see, I never ever wanted to go to South Carolina and live in Columbia.

A few days after my decision Patrick introduced me to one of his friends attending USC, named Aubrey Duggar. Aubrey and I met and it just clicked. It felt like we had known each other all of our lives. We quickly decided we would become roommates, and having that huge aspect of college become real was an enormous transformation for me. I came home and lay in my bed and thanked God for his roadblocks and all the struggles I had to endure to end up where I was supposed to be.

To this day, I could not be more thrilled with my choice of college. Everything worked out perfectly. Just like it is supposed to be. It took me a while to realize why I didn't get into North Carolina or Clemson; God wanted me at South Carolina. I have always tried to force life to fit into my plan. Because I know best, and my plan is always the correct plan . . . right? I don't think so. I always find out that it is not my plan that matters, it's His plan. That was His call, and now it will become my call.

Growing up at Fourth has helped plant the seed to start my faith journey. So many beautiful seeds scattered across my life, with all of you nourishing the seeds, watching me grow and blossom. For this I thank you. Without this church, I would have never embraced life with the same attitude, and I would have never had the faith to believe that all things were possible. And for that, I will be forever grateful. The trips to Montreat, Mexico, New Orleans, Texas, Triune, and so many other places have helped me see hatred and despair in the world. Those trips have also helped me see love and hope through new eyes. These experiences have sparked my desire to want to help change that which is wrong.

I am an extremely passionate person, and when I say I am going on a mission trip to Texas, I not only paint the house and tear down some wood; I am on top of the roof helping to apply shingles to the roof. No matter what part of the world I'm in, or what I'm doing, I give it my all. I apply this to my faith. I have felt God in so many different ways while I am with the people in this church. The candlelight services at Montreat, the Thanksgiving Day service at Reverend Duplessis's house, the streets filled with playful children in Mexico, and the late night devotions during our trips together. Not only did the trips significantly influence my life, but the people; from the Jack Huffmans to the Libby Wallins, from the Heidi Wrights to the Joe Browns. Each person in this church has shaped my life and helped make me the person I am today. Each mission trip, church service, or youth group would not be the rich experience that they are without each and every person within this church.

God has been in these places. He has led me there to experience these things, to encounter many types of people, and to learn new things. He called me there. God wanted me to learn how to love others just how Jesus came down and loved us. I have always tried to live by the phrase "Carpe Diem," or "Seize the Day." I want to live life and have a great time. But when the day is not so great, I have to remind myself that God is always there and I just have to continue to have faith to know He will make everything work out how it's supposed to. His plan!

In my life I have been blessed with other wonderful experiences to travel around the world, from the killing fields of Auschwitz to impoverished dirt-floor schools in Belize. Over the course of the last few years I have felt it has been my call to share my experiences. I want to show others the hurt and devastation in the world. I want to share my experiences and what each one has meant to me. I want to be able to make a difference and turn hate into love, despair into hope. I know with love and faith in God, I will be able to accomplish this dream, this plan, and this call. I have always had a favorite Bible verse. It is Philippians 4:13, "I can do all things through Christ who strengthens me." This verse has been able to get me through some rough times and the times when I am in doubt about what God's plan for me truly is. I try to force life upon itself. I am the one who jumps in with two feet, or who tries to put the round peg into the square hole. But I know with the divine grace of our Lord, I can do anything I set my mind to. I have to trust in God, and I have to believe that my faith will lead me in the right direction. I have to understand that MY call might not be God's call for me. With this in mind, I have to take life as it presents itself to me and live every day with the love and passion that Jesus showed 2,000 years ago.

Going to college has always been a part of my call. Going to South Carolina was never my call. Going to South Carolina was God's call, and I will embrace this challenge with elegance and dignity, because this now is my call. I now understand I cannot live my life by my call or my way, but by God's way!

I was humbled. A solitary tear trailed down my cheek. I couldn't believe that my daughter had the answer in eighteen years that I searched for, for over forty years.

Mary and I must have done something right. Our fruit were now bearing seeds of their own.

And God smiled.

Are You a Christian?

After I set out to refute Christianity intellectually and couldn't, I came to the conclusion the Bible was true and Jesus Christ was God's Son.
—JOSH MCDOWELL[45]

THE BIBLE IS A WONDROUS book filled with thousands of intriguing people and characters from over a two-thousand-year span. Although it is written so we can personally identify with most of the people and their stories to some limited capacity, there are still many I have a hard time relating to. Take Joseph, the husband of Mary for example. If I found out my fiancée was pregnant and she and I hadn't consummated our love, I'd be out the door so fast it wouldn't have time to swing back and hit me in the rear.

Or what about Pharaoh? That guy was all decked out like a modern-day rock star sporting Rolexes and Bentleys while chilling in the Biltmore Mansion. I'm just glad my Timex keeps ticking and my 200,000-mile Chevy Suburban still cranks when the temperature dips below 40.

How about Abraham? Poised with a gleaming dagger in his hand, ready to strike down his son on a pile of brush so he can then cremate the remains and send them as a burnt offering to God. I don't think so. Or Noah? Building a big boat in my backyard would have had the homeowners association revoking my membership and placing a lien on my house. I don't even have a boat trailer. Or Jonah? Now that was a story to tell my friends. "Hey guys, sorry I missed the game on Saturday. I was swallowed by a whale." I can't even stand to take a fish off the hook. Or Lazarus? How can I identify with a guy that was lying in a tomb for a few days with his skin rotting away just to be brought back to life by some nomad prophet? There wouldn't be enough Oil of Olay to restore my skin back to a healthy, silky sheen. That must have been a scene.

And what about Jesus, the Son of God? I have a hard time identifying with a guy whose mother was impregnated by the Holy Spirit. The kids in the neighborhood would never let that one go without a few jabs. And it's hard to even fathom being nailed to a cross and having the power to release yourself, but instead bearing all of mankind's sins for eternity. That sure is a heavy load. My sins alone are enough to break my back.

But Paul? Now that's a guy I can identify with. He was everything anti-Christian. He would have never considered himself a Christian under any circumstance. He was all about money, power, and personal achievement in the secular world. Now that sounds familiar. Then on a dusty road he was struck down and blinded by the power of God. He shed everything that he was, including his old name. There was the old Saul, and now here was the new Paul, a man with two distinctively different lives. He labeled himself a follower of Christ and wouldn't stop until he let everyone know where he stood. He became a Christian. Yes, that's a guy I can relate to.

: : : : : :

"Are you a Christian?" The question hung in the air like a half-filled balloon grasping for altitude. I was still working at OMG and developing my faith as a new-found Christian.

After my just-introduced new colleague asked me the question, she didn't look at me. Her eyes, as black as coal, were fixed on the flickering white stripes separating the lanes on Highway 8 on our way toward a small California town. Strands of her straight black hair swept across her slender, attractive face.

What an odd question, I thought. In fact, no one had ever asked me that, other than the Bible thumpers in Lynchburg. It had been a long time since someone drilled me about my love for God and my faith in Jesus Christ. When I used to be like her, I was inquisitive about those people who I had now become.

Helen had picked me up by the luggage carousel at the San Diego airport about an hour earlier. I was just elected to the board of a national association and the next meeting was in California the following Tuesday. I first saw her talking on her cell phone next to a group of weary travelers. I had never seen her before so I wasn't sure my suspicion was correct. When we introduced ourselves to each other I couldn't get past her eyes. They were as dark as ebony. I had never seen that before, especially on a face as pretty as hers. As the old saying goes, "The eyes are the windows to the soul." What he meant was one's eyes reveal hidden emotions and attitudes about a person. With Helen, I couldn't see past the window pane.

We jumped in the shiny black rental car and drove east for our thirty-minute ride. Since I was the new board member and Helen was the board president, she wanted to know more about me, as much as half an hour could disclose. That wouldn't be a problem; I was well versed on me. I led her on a journey through Chapel Hill on the way to South Carolina. It appeared my work history sounded much more interesting than it actually was. People have always seemed interested about the ins and outs of the entertainment business.

The conversation turned to music. Of course she got an earful about our recording studio, our deal with EMI, big-time musicians I had associated with, and all the commercial stuff eager ears want to hear. When people are on the outside of the music industry, talking to someone on the inside always seemed impressive. Helen had just joined a band. She was nearly fifty but looked like she was about thirty-five. She was clearly passionate about music. Although Helen was driving the car, I was clearly in the driver's seat. We talked about her new favorite group, The Kings of Leon. Well, of course I'm "real good friends" with the attorney that put their deal together in Nashville. If she threw out a name, I was like Kevin Bacon reducing the six degrees of separation to three or four, or maybe even one.

We rode, Helen in her black leather jacket and me with my black cotton pull-over. She asked, I answered. We rode.

She inquired about music publishing and how our music company dealt with it. I told her the story of Chasen, how we signed them, worked the project, then were in the position to field offers from the majors. She seemed fascinated, or maybe it was just my fascination of telling the story again.

"The band had a #2 song on the Christian CHR carts. It was a Christian rock band that had some cross-over potential," I said with reserved pride. I was hoping to keep Pandora's Box closed.

Silence.

She kept her eyes on the road.

I felt compelled to explain the Christian music industry even though she didn't ask.

Silence.

The quiet was deafening. It got the best of me.

"You know the Fray, right?" I probed.

"Sure."

"They're a Christian band. In fact they're just a group of Christian praise and worship leaders from Colorado who had that one hit that propelled them to international stardom," I couldn't stop the explanation. "Based on that hit, they were able to roll out a pretty successful run of top mainstream hits. But they started as a Christian band . . . really. What about U2?" I knew her response before she answered, just like a good lawyer. "They're a Christian band. Just listen to their lyrics. They got their start in Ireland and parlayed it to global mega-band success. I guess they're technically not a Christian band but they are a band of Christians."

Without cause, I was in a battle with myself about defending Christian music. Or was I in a battle with myself? I was still not always comfortable with my new-found badge of honor when having to explain my stance and how God changed my life. *Christian* was my new label. I grew more eager to talk about my faith, but I was young in my understanding of the gospel so I didn't want to falsely represent Christianity. I had no idea who she worshiped, what she worshiped, or if she worshiped anything at all.

Helen kept driving. She stared straight ahead.

Christian, Christian, Christian, Christian, Christian, Christian, Christian, Christian, Christian, Christian, Christian, Christian, Christian, Christian, and Christian, I kept thinking to myself. *Okay, I'm done. Great first impression!*

Silence.

After a few moments, without any prodding by me, Helen revealed the obvious. "I'm not a Christian."

Silence.

Like many non-believers, she had a problem with the authenticity of the Bible. Having recently read a book on the reliability of the Bible, I knew I was cautiously ready to answer any and all questions she may be pondering. I was prepared to convert her instantly. *I will win*, I thought.

As Helen brought up topics that caused her to disbelieve Christ's reality, I was surprised and at a disadvantage. She brought a brick to a pillow fight and I found myself inadequately prepared for the moment. My feather pillow had no bite. I was earnestly ready to share my faith, but embarrassingly, I could not string together the words to adequately defend my God.

Conversation ensued about the Muslim faith and other world religions. I maintained a steady dialogue but I knew in my heart that I should have been better prepared. On a thirty-minute drive that felt like four hours and thirty minutes, I had the opportunity of a lifetime. I desperately wanted to remove from her eyes the same blinders that had kept my soul from being pierced by God's love. I wanted to help save her life. I wanted to share with her the wonder that had radically changed my worldview. I wanted her to see the light of Truth.

I knew, as we would talk later into the evening, that her questions were being framed by my belief. Her inquisition was sincere and not damning like some non-believers'. Helen wanted to know more about my relationship with God. Perhaps I opened the door for her and she saw a peek of the light and wanted to see more.

I wished I was better equipped, but as fate would have it, all that was meant to be revealed was revealed. I believe Helen helped me more than I helped her. I knew next time I needed to be better prepared. For the first time I was face to face with my uncomfortable responsibility as a Christian, a label I loathed but was ironically transformed into, just like Paul.

"Are you a Christian?"

"I am."

Sometimes I Cry

Give me your eyes for just one second
Give me your eyes so I can see
Everything that I keep missing
Give me your love for humanity
Give me your arms for the broken hearted
Ones that are far beyond my reach
Give me your heart for the ones forgotten
Give me your eyes so I can see
—BRANDON HEATH[46]

SOMETIMES I CRY.

I cry for the human condition. I cry because so many people lack sympathy and compassion. We drive by those helpless people on the streets that have no place to go, and look away in the opposite direction. They have no home, nobody waiting on them for dinner, no warm bed greeting them at night, only a cold piece of concrete under the Main Street Bridge or an abandoned house scheduled for demolition. On most nights they're lucky to have a can of sardines and a pack of crackers for their daily meal. We pay no attention because we have more important things to do—*those people* cramp our style and don't fit into our busy routine.

On our way to church to worship God, we drive by the buildings and shelters that welcome the homeless and the hungry without even considering the loneliness and suffering trapped within their walls. We sit still for an hour and listen to the well-spoken minister deliver the powerful Word of God, how Jesus helped the helpless, how we should walk in His footsteps, and how we need to recognize His plan for our lives. On our way home, we drive right by the same buildings again, eager to get home for Sunday lunch, but how often do we stop? How often do we say "Use me"? How often do we carve time out of our precious schedule and say, "God, use me as Your instrument of love"? How often do we tithe our resources to the needy and broken in addition to our weekly check in the offering plate? How often do we act on the simple question, "What would Jesus do?"

Sometimes I cry.

: : : : : :

In a packed fellowship hall, the church was holding a combined summer adult Sunday school series instead of the usual smaller groups held in rooms throughout the church building. We were exploring the beauty of the Psalms. On that particular morning we were fully engaged with the story of the Good Samaritan. The class leader lobbed out a question something along the lines of, "Who is or was somebody you could think of that has helped others they didn't even know with selfless love?"

A number of names echoed through the room, such as the obvious Mother Teresa, Nelson Mandela, and congregation members who go above and beyond their normal obligations. I was listening for someone to say my name but no one did. My vanity had no bounds, not even for approval of selfless service. I could only shake my head at my own absurdity. During a lull in the responses I figured I'd toss one out: "Bill Gates."

A few heads turned in my direction, knowing that if it was an answer from "Gene," there would certainly be some sort of rambling follow-up.

"Look at that guy," I started. "Here is a man who built arguably the largest and wealthiest business empire in the history of mankind from scratch. He now chooses to give the majority of his financial wealth away through the Bill and Melinda Gates Foundation as well as challenging others of the world's billionaires like Warren Buffett to do the same. Gates gets criticized sometimes for how he gives his money away, but hey, it's a private foundation, it's his money. How can anyone criticize his efforts when he is single-handedly doing more for healing this world through health programs, education, and global research than anyone else? He will never meet the millions he helps but he does it for the good of all mankind. Now that's a guy following the steps of Jesus."

I heard no verbal responses but I did see a few head nods. A couple of moments later a hand was raised across the room. My astute fellow church member began to speak and turned his head in my direction as he completed his comment. "Bill Gates is an atheist you know."

"Bill Gates is an atheist?" I responded as I tried to shake his statement out of my head. "What difference does that make? It has nothing to do with the question that was asked. I don't know whether Bill Gates is an atheist, an agnostic, or a Muslim, but we 'Christians' can learn a lot from him. His actions are more Christlike than most anyone I know. He *is* the Good Samaritan."

For some reason, that general observation about Bill Gates's faith or lack of faith never settled with me. Whether or not he is a Christian wasn't the point; his actions were certainly to be admired as he represented true love for his brothers and sisters around the world. He was practicing Christian love. Bill Gates clearly loved his neighbor, a command Jesus required of us all.

Much of the Bill Gates atheist discussion swirled around old interviews with David Frost and Walter Isaacson where Gates said, "The specific elements of Christianity are not something I'm a huge believer in."[47] He was later quoted as saying, "Just in terms of allocation of time resources, religion is not very efficient. There's a lot more I could be doing on a Sunday morning."[48]

I certainly couldn't argue with his second point; Gates could use his time to be making more money on Sunday morning to give away to the poor. Whether or not he goes to church wasn't the issue. What resonated with me was how he helps others with selfless love. Sometimes the church isn't the cure for a problem; it's the cause. Much of the religion being taught in churches around the world misses the mark on the core requirements of us as Christians. Bill Gates may not believe in God or Jesus Christ, but many of his actions have definitely appeared to be that of a Christian. He truly seemed to care for the least of God's people, those who were wallowing in poverty and oppression around the world.

: : : : : :

As our group unloaded from the rickety bus in Monterrey, Mexico, I began to appreciate the change Bill Gates was attempting to effect. The stench in the air as the bus door clanged open was pungent and overwhelming. The city trash dump we were driven to was a rancid cesspool of festering filth and disease; there were piles of all imaginable refuse for as far as the eye could see. It was an odd place to be spending an afternoon, not to mention a peculiar place to schedule lunch.

The James Fund, the charitable arm of Family Christian Stores, led countless mission trips to the forsaken area. Steve, a man cut from the cloth of Paul, was the leader on the trip and had spent many days at the trash heap over the years.

The Premier Foundation was a loyal supporter of the James Fund, an organization called to look after the widow and orphan.

Their directive came straight from James 1:27: "Religion that God our Father accepts as pure and faultless is this: to look after orphans and widows in their distress and to keep oneself from being polluted by the world" (NIV).

A part of my responsibility was to go and see firsthand how Premier Foundation's granted dollars were being used. It was important to make sure our valuable resources were being used to glorify Christ. I had no doubt the James Fund was a trusted steward of our gifts. Still, I needed to see their work firsthand; but I certainly didn't expect to be unloaded at a trash pile called Rio Three.

The summer Mexico heat was sweltering outside, which made the rotting food and garbage even more disgustingly pungent. The garbage dump was about a mile long and meandered along the curves of a docile river. Only a month earlier, torrential rains caused the calm river to transform into a raging rapid. It wouldn't have been an issue except for the fact that about 150 people were living on and in the dump. It was a sad and unfathomable scene scattered with despair. My heart broke as we walked from shack to shack inviting the residents of the squatter's village to lunch in the lean-to at the entrance of the community.

Their homes were built from whatever could be salvaged from the daily deposits of trash. Springs from a mattress were used as a gate while anything thick enough to hold out the rain was propped up as a roof. A scrawny horse was tied to a tree on the muddy road along the homes.

Home, I thought. *These are people's homes.*

There were children laughing and playing around the dump. It was a mind-boggling scene. My only explanation to myself was that they didn't know how bad they had it. But, if they had love from their parents and their neighbors, then that was a lot more than many people in my own community had. I kept speculating on their situation as a way to rationalize the truth of their existence.

I walked ahead of our mission group trying to compose my thoughts as I wondered where humanity was. I tried to connect the dots, asking myself how the God of all the people in my church in South Carolina was the same God of all the people living in what looked like hell; it was only lacking a burning lake of sulfur. I couldn't understand how this could happen, how people could actually live in the middle of a trash dump.

"Hola," someone beckoned in Spanish as we stopped at another shanty. A young girl came out who appeared to be about thirteen or fourteen years old. She was holding a new-born child, an innocent little baby girl birthed about two weeks earlier . . . in the garbage dump! The next information I received put me on overload. The young girl wasn't the baby's sister; she was the baby's mother. Those two precious children of God were the poster children for poverty, birth control, and sorrow. The mother had both conceived the child and given birth to the infant in the surroundings that would cause the most callous hearts to cry.

I was angry. I have always loved children, especially newborns. They are the essence of God's existence. It was the first time in my life I actually wished a child hadn't been born. It was different watching a three- or four-year-old running around and frolicking; but seeing an innocent newborn in that environment broke my heart. Instead of ogling at the baby, I had to walk away to hide my anger. *This child has no chance*, I cried to myself. *This should never happen, anywhere.*

If possible, I would have snatched up the little girl and brought her back to South Carolina before she had the chance to comprehend where she was living, where she was welcomed into this world. The innocent and defenseless newborn had no choice whether to be born or not, nor did she have the privilege of choosing her parents. She was not a member of the lucky birth club, like the kids born in middle or upper-middle class America with everything at their fingertips. She was not the child of Bill Gates or Donald Trump with a promising future, a warm bed, and healthy food. There would be no golf courses, iPads, or a car at her sixteenth birthday. No Christmas presents from Target under the tree. There would be one meal a day if she was lucky. She was destined for a hard uphill battle that would quite possibly lead to drugs, rape, prostitution, or even slavery . . . if she lived that long. She was a child born into utter poverty, desperate for a way out; she just didn't know it yet. Everything was stacked against her, everything except for the persistent effort of the James Fund.

Many of the children who lived in Rio Three were being assisted by a ministry that the James Fund supported. They made sure the children went to school so they would have a chance at breaking the cycle of horrible poverty. After Steve explained how the organizations worked together to look after the people of this impoverished area, calm entered my heart. I knew the resources we granted to the James Fund were being used for pure loving service to those who needed it most. Our money was making a difference. Although I cried when I saw the real circumstances of life on the trash pile, God smiled at the Christian resolve of the missionaries and our group's dedication to help our brothers and sisters. There were no boundaries of nationality when I looked into the eyes of the residents of the garbage dump; they were my brothers and sisters.

Our next stop in Monterrey was at an orphanage built by a family of missionaries years before. It was a huge expanse of land with fields for playing in, gardens for planting crops, and solid buildings providing secure sleeping quarters—a world apart from the trash heap just miles down the road.

A blessing of a lifetime was in store for our small group of volunteers from all across America. One of the volunteers in our group worked for a national discount shoe store chain, and they had donated hundreds of new shoes for distribution to orphans in Monterrey.

After lunch, all the children swarmed to the open-air chapel-pavilion near the entrance to the property. Our mission leaders arranged for buckets of water to be placed by two brown folding chairs. The children came up one by one and were seated with their feet dangling over the ground. All of the volunteers took turns as we would kneel by the chairs.

My turn came. The sweet young girl sat on the chair wearing a pretty shirt, beige pants, and a reserved smile. I slowly took each leg and removed her tattered shoes. I placed her feet in the bucket and gently washed each foot. I felt an overwhelming joy. I had never washed anyone's feet in that capacity; it had been only my own daughters' little feet in our bathtub. When I washed the young girl's feet I was humbling myself before God to truly serve His child. A sheepish grin formed on her face, and mine too.

With the shoes separated by size, she pointed to the pair she wanted. I dried her feet, put a new pair of socks on her, and slid on the new shoes over her toes and around her heels. It was a simple gift, but by the look of her smile it was perhaps the best present she had ever received. The children at the orphanage rarely received anything new, much less new shoes. I had never realized how important a new pair of kicks could be.

When the oldest boy finally took his turn in the seat, it was apparent we weren't prepared for a young man with size twelve feet. There were no shoes that would fit him. His face dropped as he tried to hide his disappointment. In a quick second, one of the members of our group recognized the issue and gladly offered his slightly worn Nikes as a gift to the young man. His face beamed . . . so did the face of the boy.

We were taken to numerous orphanages throughout Monterrey. With each stop, Steve explained how The James Fund, with the help of the Premier Foundation and other organizations, made a difference. It was even greater validation that God had me where He wanted me. I was able to use my gifts to glorify Him in a loving and caring way I never dreamed possible. I truly felt like the luckiest man in the world, although I consistently didn't feel worthy of the position.

Why was God so good to me by placing me in the position at Premier? I would keep asking myself.

I had let God down so many times in the past; I couldn't understand why He rewarded me with the best job opportunity I could ever imagine. For some reason He granted me with the job of a lifetime, one where I would stretch my own boundaries of love. In my new calling, I was making a real difference in the lives of so many.

Facts and figures often become overwhelming. When I first heard that there were approximately 147 million orphans in the world, it was easy to close my eyes and say, "That number is so big, there is no way I can make a dent in the global crisis." But then I met Stephie, a young girl living at an orphanage in Monterrey, another one of the facilities that the James Fund supported. Invariably, there would always be a connection between a missionary and a certain child. Steve told me it can't be orchestrated, it just happens. And when it happened, I knew. For me, it was Stephie. She was a confident eight-year-old girl who walked with perfect posture, poise, and strong confidence. As I looked into her green eyes, I could see hope. Those 147 million orphans became one. My heart rejoiced with the knowledge that we, as a community of faith, could make a dent in the crisis, but we had to do it one child at a time. It would have to be one willing family at a time reaching out to one lonely parentless child at a time.

With every new country, and every new community, circumstances invariably brought me to tears. The human condition is sometimes more desperate and hopeless than our minds can conceive, filled with abandoned, abused, and lost children. But we can provide hope. It doesn't have to be as extreme as the young college kids who relocate to Mexico and commit their lives to rebuilding an orphanage, or as radical as moving an entire family south of the border to serve as house parents to a half-dozen wayward teenage girls. Hope is available for everyone to give, and it can be given through a drastic and radical measure or simply a donation to a worthwhile charity. Hope can be given by providing a shoulder to cry on laced with a few words of encouragement or it can be given by serving as a mentor to someone in need. We have to be ready to hear how God wants us to provide that hope.

It is only with an intentional heart and willing mind that we can effect change for the good of those less fortunate. Change for the better won't happen by itself like a self-correcting Microsoft spell check. It's more like the old Smith Corona typewriters that required removing one cartridge ribbon and inserting a new correcting cartridge ribbon to fix the error. It required intentional effort to correct what was wrong. Fixing this world is no different. It will take intentional effort that will lead us to the land of many tears. But tears of sadness can be turned into tears of joy—we just can't be afraid to cry.

So What's Next?

Everyday is a chance for a new stance
Like every song is the beginning of a new dance
And everyone of us was made to reflect the light
And glorify the most high so bright
We got one world 'til it's time to fly
So it's one love 'til we say goodbye
—Toby Mac[49]

So what's next?

George Rogers, a close friend of mine who was the 1980 Heisman Trophy winner and the first pick in the 1981 NFL Draft, always said he believed God gave us two eyes in the front of our head so we would look ahead instead of continually looking at where we were. I have tended to agree with much of that philosophy; however, I believe that our past offers invaluable lessons for our future.

Fellow college classmate and the greatest basketball player in the history of the game, Michael Jordan, also subscribed to looking ahead, but he found great value in the past. If Jordan missed a shot, he wouldn't dwell on the fact that he should have made the easy bucket; instead he chose to look at the miscue as a learning experience. He would try to understand why he missed the shot and correct the error the next time down the floor. He had an uncanny ability to not dwell on the past; rather, he used the experience to learn from the past and apply what he learned to better prepare himself for the future. He usually made the shot the next time he was presented with similar circumstances. It was a characteristic I have tried to employ. We should learn from our past but not live in it.

My life has been filled with countless mistakes and miscues. For years they were marks of disappointment I dwelled on; I now view them as gifts. Every experience I have lived through, I can now look at as a learning opportunity and a precious gift.

Many of those hard lessons came in the form of real life experiences that have enriched my soul and given me a new vision for my future.

: : : : : :

Montell was a drug dealer. He was also a friend. The secular entertainment industry was like a magnet for people from all walks of life, like a moth to the flame. Montell came into my life with a desire to do good with the money he made from selling drugs. His smile was infectious and his front tooth was plated with gold that shone when he talked. At the time, I didn't know where he earned his cash; I was told it was from legitimate business ventures. Nonetheless, I could add one plus one, so perhaps it was simply a desire not to know where all of his money came from.

Montell had a good heart, but he was plagued with easy money to support him and his family. Easy money became an addiction even though he was trying to find a way out and become a legitimate businessman. He felt that associating himself with legitimate business people would help facilitate his own transformation. Montell knew I was on a quest to find God's truth; that made him even more attracted to me and my company.

During an abnormally difficult financial run for me, while trying to provide for my wife and two young daughters, I became trapped.

I needed a lot of money and I needed it fast to help support my family and those around me and to fulfill my various obligations that were bearing down. As a last resort I called Montell.

I met him in a dimly lit parking lot with only a few cars scattered about. I jumped in his vehicle and we rolled to his one-story house.

Walking into his home was like strolling into a Cheech and Chong movie. The living room was filled with a cloud of smoke from the tightly rolled blunts. A mound of marijuana was piled on the coffee table and the glimmer from a handgun could be seen peeking out near the table. A box of baggies was opened and sitting next to the weed, right next to the scale.

We weren't alone. Another character was sitting on the couch with his bloodshot eyes barely visible through the slits of his eyelids while he watched a basketball game on the wall-sized television. Yet another person was roaming around the house doing whatever he was doing. It was like a bad Dr. Dre rap video.

I felt a bit uneasy but knew Montell, so I felt reasonably safe. He smiled and laughed as he welcomed me into his home, his gold tooth catching my eye as he spoke.

"You want to smoke?" he asked.

"No, I'm good," I slowly replied with appreciation at the offer. "Thanks anyway."

The FUBU-clothed guy on the couch looked at me with suspicion at turning down the offer to get high.

"You sure?" the guy said.

"Yeah, I'm sure. Thanks."

The other person came out of the kitchen rolling a wheel with 24-inch spoke rims.

"You want to buy some rims?" he asked with a devilish smile.

"No, I'm good."

"Check 'em out. They're tight," he pressed like an award-winning salesman.

"I appreciate it. I don't think those are for me."

"All right, cool." He rolled the tire back into the kitchen, mumbling something to himself.

Montell invited me to his back bedroom where the enormous steel safe occupied the corner of his sleeping chamber. It was proudly situated right next to his king-size bed. I felt like I was watching *Scarface* with Al Pacino and I was oddly featured in the movie.

Montell rolled the dial on the safe. Right, left, right. Click. He turned the large handle. It clicked again. He pulled open the door to reveal a significant amount of cash and other interesting items. He pulled out a few stacks of the worn bills and counted them out. "Here ya go." He handed it to me with his gold-toothed smile.

I stuffed the cash into my pockets then hugged Montell.

"Thanks, man," I said. "I'll get this back to you as agreed."

"I'm not worried about that. I'm glad I could help," he chuckled with his ever-present upbeat nature.

Montell wasn't a loan shark demanding 30 percent interest. In fact, he wasn't even worried about any interest. "I got you covered, Gene."

He shut the safe door and spun the dial. I walked back into the living room with softball-sized bulges in my pockets. Two stoned guys were now sitting on the couch looking at me as if I was the sheep and they were wolves, or it may have just been my imagination. I knew they had been blazing on the marijuana for some time now, and who knows what else, increasing my paranoia.

They asked me again if I wanted to get high and I graciously declined. The now discounted tires and silver rims were offered again. I declined. Montell drove me back to my car. I felt safe when I was alone with him, but when I hopped into my vehicle by myself the paranoia set in again. I knew the guys on the couch knew. That made me uneasy. The drive from the parking lot to my house was a white-knuckle thrill ride, looking in my rearview and side view mirrors more than I was focusing on the road ahead of me. I took an unusual route to my house, constantly checking that I wasn't being followed. I had done nothing illegal; I had nothing to worry about. I was merely accepting a loan from a friend of mine, just like the countless loans I personally made to others. My fear was being jacked by Snoop Dogg and the Notorious B.I.G., a couple of characters I knew nothing about. I made it home safe without incident.

Over the course of a couple of years, I made regular payments to Montell, reducing the principal amount of the loan. Times continued to get tight and as we were considering closing OMG, the burden of his and other loans began to mount as I faced an uncertain future. I wanted to pay him back ASAP but couldn't figure out how to do it. I owed a lot of people a lot of money and a lot of other people owed me a lot of money. I had been generous, floating loans out to friends in a bind when times were prosperous for me. It was a vicious cycle. If everyone had repaid the cash they owed me and the company, my obligations would have been made much easier to meet.

In a stressful moment, my Blackberry rang. It was Montell.

"Hey, what's up man?" I cheerfully shot, wondering what the purpose of the call was.

"Not much, all is good," he cheerfully returned. "So, Gene, you know that loan?"

"Yeah?" I winced.

"I'm forgiving the debt. You don't owe me anything."

I was humbly silent.

"Listen, it's all good. We're square," he continued.

"Montell, I don't know what . . . I don't know what to say. I appreciate it, but why are you doing this?"

"The Bible tells us to forgive our debts, so that's what I'm doing. I'm forgiving the debt."

Montell had turned his life over to Christ. He had stopped selling drugs and went from living a lifestyle flush with cash and whatever toy he wanted to buy for himself, to an honest living and struggling to just get by. Montell was starting at square one. If anyone could not afford to forgive the debt, it was him. He was having trouble paying the rent and keeping the lights on, but he was following the Scripture and felt it was something he had to do. Even with the terrible financial position he found himself in, he seemed happier and more joyful than I could ever remember. He was thankful in his poverty and put all of his faith in God that He would deliver him from his circumstances. He instantly became a role model of faith.

I hung up the phone in utter disbelief. I was humbled to tears at the gracious gesture of a man who was giving all he had and making every effort to follow Christ and correct his life from years of sin.

I immediately made a list of everyone I could think of who personally owed me money. I began dialing the phone and doing exactly what Montell had done for me. I began to forgive the thousands of dollars that were owed to me by others. I figured if Montell could do it, so could I. The domino effect was significant and a loving offering to God.

Montell was my teacher. I learned from him one of Christ's simple principles in action: "And forgive us our debts, as we also have forgiven our debtors." As I continued to learn, I put the principle into action for myself. Forgiving the debts owed me was incredibly rewarding. It not only warmed my heart with each phone call, it relieved an ever-present burden and animosity I had for those people who were not repaying me their obligation.

It was awe-inspiring being the recipient of Montell's gracious love. He could afford it the least but stood tall and truly made God smile the most. Montell had just taught me a valuable life lesson.

: : : : : :

The lessons didn't stop coming.

I was living in a quandary of not being able to make ends meet and needing sizable and reliable transportation. My sedan was small for the children and not a good representation for driving around potentially high-wealth clients. I approached an acquaintance who owned a car dealership and who Mary and I had purchased a number of vehicles from through the years. He was an entrepreneur himself and understood the challenges of building a business.

He graciously agreed to purchase some of my company stock with the caveat that I would, in turn, use some of the cash to purchase a vehicle from him and solve one of my needs. I bought the vehicle of my dreams, a brand new, shiny, black GMC Yukon. I tinted the windows and installed a DVD player with an abnormally large screen for my young daughters. I had to fight the temptation of calling Montell and purchasing twenty-four-inch spoke rims for my new ride. I knew this was a vehicle I would have for many years to come. It was paid in full; thus, no burdening monthly payments and an excellent representation for current and potential clients.

I had driven the stylish Yukon for a few months and only accumulated 9,000 miles on it when the lack of salary crept up on me like a rogue wave. After heart-wrenching consideration and discussions with Mary, my course of action was abundantly evident. I needed to sell the Yukon and get reacquainted with my Mitsubishi. As I needed the money sooner than later, CarMax offered a significant amount for the almost new GMC.

Although it was difficult to part with the vehicle my family and I loved so much, it taught me another valuable lesson. I learned that material items are temporary and we should never attach ourselves to or claim to "love" any riches of this world. After the fact, I was abundantly confident that all of this timing was ordained by God. He knew what I needed when I needed it and was always there to provide for my family and me. The money I received from the sale helped sustain my family while I was still building OMG and opting out of salary.

Manna came in many forms, even wrapped up in the polished steel and beige leather of a shiny, new, black Yukon.

: : : : : :

Sometimes it's hard for people to say "thank you" and "you're welcome." The gesture is simple but can often be awkward. In a grocery store outside of New Orleans on the day before Thanksgiving, I was taught yet another lesson in how to show loving gratitude.

About eight of our mission team, all dressed in blue Presbyterian Disaster Assistance shirts, wandered through an upscale grocery store in search of some items to bring to E.J.'s house. Since it was Thanksgiving, we wanted to spend an hour or so with E.J. to let him know how much we appreciated him. The store was bustling with last-minute shoppers searching for the plumpest Butterball and the perfect bottle of wine.

The groceries were being moved along the black conveyer belt toward the scanner. Our group of high school kids, a newly ordained minister, and I were laughing and smiling amid the stern focus of the other holiday shoppers. We were dirty and sweaty from a long day of work, a sharp contrast to the other clean and well-dressed customers.

The clerk began to scan the items.

The beautifully manicured woman standing behind us in the line at the register looked in my direction. "Are you here on vacation?" she asked as she intently wondered.

"We are," I happily responded. "We have a group of about fifteen people down here from South Carolina. We thought it would be the perfect way to spend Thanksgiving, rebuilding some houses and a school, while we sleep on a church floor." I chuckled a bit about the church floor comment.

She looked away from me for a moment as she softly said under her breath, "I can't believe people are still coming down here to help."

It had been over four years since the storm. "There's still a lot of work to do," I said.

She looked at the cashier. "Put their groceries on my bill."

Shocked, I quickly replied, "No, you don't have to do that."

"I know I don't. But I can and I will!" she demanded.

"No, really, we got this."

"Put their food on my bill," she directed at the cashier as if there would be no further discussion.

I knew when the battle was lost, so I nodded my head to her and simply said, "Thank you." However, it wasn't me who was thanking her, it was her thanking us.

I put my paint-covered arm around her as I fought my tears. I could tell her tears were moments away as she keenly began to understand why we were spending a family holiday in her own backyard. She knew it was because we loved.

It was a moment I would never forget. But more importantly it was an indelible scene played out in front of a half dozen of our church youth. The exchange would be engraved on their hearts as they continued to plod forward on their journey of truly living the life of a Christian.

I had always been the one to arbitrarily give to others and ask for nothing in return. I enjoyed buying movie tickets for the person in front of me in the line with sheer delight at simply giving, or randomly helping a stranger on the street. I always told my girls, "I'm just paying it forward." But it got a bit uncomfortable for me to be on the receiving end of the arbitrary kindness. It was a challenge to simply accept the kindness and move on, but it was a lesson I needed to be taught.

We grabbed our bags and walked toward the sliding glass doors. My oldest daughter, Caroline, could see how the interaction humbled me. She nudged me on the arm. "Hey, Dad. She was just paying it forward."

: : : : : :

We live in the moment. We can't live in the past. Nor can we live in the future. We can learn from the past. We can hope for the future.

The old saying "hindsight is 20/20" gives us a glimpse into the wonders of how God carries us through life. Even when I was not actively participating in God's life, the gift of hindsight allowed me to see how God was always caring for me in my life; I only had to open my eyes and reflect. Holding me, guiding me, and gracing me with His love and the abundant gift of experience. Only now can I look back and clearly see my faults, sins, and spiritual ignorance that I gratefully cherish as gifts from God. Only now can I see how and when God spoke to me through life. I was blind but now I see. Only now can I be thankful for my disappointments and failures and enjoy the blessings that my shortcomings taught me . . . and are still teaching me.

My misguided arrogance and ego that led me to believe that I was the ruler of my own destiny was simply being misguided by self. We are not here to gain personal accolades. We are here to truly reflect the love that God has for us; we are here to reflect His light. We are here to be His instrument of love as John 15:12 (NIV) illustrates: "My command is this: Love each other as I have loved you." Keeping this command in mind with each precious breath gives new hope for the world, a roadmap that leads us to love and nurture the person living in the house next to us as well as the AIDS-stricken child in Africa that hasn't eaten in three days. We must love all people as Christ did and does. We must lend a helping hand, shout with a powerful voice, and stand without fear as we live the life God calls each one of us to live. It is not easy— it is required.

We are all blessed with rich experiences. We all make mistakes. The challenge is to not look at them as wrong moves or disappointments—the true opportunity is to look at them as gifts, special presents, important blessings from God. The mistakes in our lives are information we can use to help implement God's plan and create a better world for our brothers and sisters.

There is no better gift than to be able to look back on our lives and know we have left a positive mark on the hearts of others, a mark that encouraged someone to repeat the cycle of living a life for the glory of God.

It's up to us, you and me—let's do it!

That's what's next!

I Want to be like George Bailey

I want to leave the world a better place for me having been here.
—JAMES NAISMITH[50]

IT'S A WONDERFUL LIFE IS my favorite movie.[51]

It is a compelling story of a young man played by Jimmy Stewart, George Bailey, who lived a truly blessed life. He has big dreams of leaving his hometown of Bedford Falls and traveling the world before he goes off to college. He has his life planned out to the letter. With big eyes and a vision for the future, he tells everyone, "I want to do something big. Something important." But as life's circumstances prevail, George never leaves his hometown due to a string of unforeseen events.

Without even knowing it, George has a positive impact on everyone his life touches, starting a domino effect that helps make his town a wonderful place to live. He's a guy that always does the right thing even to his own detriment, no matter the ramifications.

As a child, George jumps into an icy lake to save his brother's life. His brother, Harry, goes on to become a war hero by saving the lives of an entire transport filled with soldiers. Because of the cold water, George loses hearing in one of his ears.

After George's boss at the drug store, Mr. Gower, receives a telegram that his son has died, the grieving man mistakenly fills a prescription with poison. The error would have killed the sick child for whom the medicine was meant. George, who witnessed the mistake, intentionally doesn't deliver the prescription, which ultimately saves the child's life. Mr. Gower beats George when he finds out that he did not deliver the prescription, but then tearfully thanks George when he finds out it would have killed the patient.

When George's father dies, he gives up his dream of going to college, instead choosing to take over the family business, a struggling community building and loan. As a downturn in the economy forces a run on his business, he sacrifices and gives away his honeymoon money, loaning it to his clients, calming their fears. His loving wife, Mary, supports him, knowing that he did the admirable thing for his neighbors. George again gives up another dream of traveling the world with his new bride. He always does the right thing, always sacrificing his own dreams for the good of the whole.

Then the story turns when a mean-spirited bank mogul, Mr. Potter, aims to take over George's business. As an act of evil kindness, Mr. Potter tries to hire George and absorb the building and loan instead of continuing to compete with the righteous Mr. Bailey. The young, tall, and handsome George Bailey at first agrees to the deal that would pay him more than he ever imagined, ten times his current salary. But George soon realizes, merely seconds after shaking Mr. Potter's clammy hand, that the offer would place him in a position of working for the devil himself. He turns Mr. Potter's offer down. This is where it gets interesting.

Mr. Potter seizes an opportunity to take advantage of a simple but terrible financial mistake made by George's business partner, Uncle Billy. Potter witnesses Uncle Billy misplacing an enormous amount of the company's money. The growing building and loan, as a result of the error, becomes a business on the verge of bankruptcy. Mr. Potter attempts to seize the chance to have complete power and control over the town. The mistake would offer the crusty old profiteer an opportunity to destroy George's business, his family, and everything he stands for in life, as well as send George to prison. Potter suggests to George that by virtue of his life insurance policy, the young man would be worth more dead than alive; George Bailey painfully decides to take his own life and jump off the Bedford Falls Bridge into the icy river below.

Sometimes I feel like George Bailey, when things don't seem to go my way and there's no way out of a tough situation. The pile seems to only get bigger, bigger, and bigger. Fears mount and pressure throbs with every desperate breath. There seems to be nowhere to turn for the answers I so desperately need. "Am I making the right decisions? How do I get out of this situation? Would the world be better off without me? Do I make a positive difference in anybody's life but my own? Do I even make a difference in my life? How do I know if I make a positive difference? How will people remember me when I am gone? Will I leave this world a better place by having lived?" I turn to God and pray for a voice, a sign, an epiphany, a moment of clarity, a life preserver . . . anything!

Nothing.

Sometimes I feel like George Bailey.

As fate paints the picture, a bumbling yet gentle guardian angel named Clarence rescues George and gives him the most wonderful Christmas gift anyone could ever receive . . . a look at life . . . as if he were never born.

While journeying through a Bedford Falls void of George's existence, Clarence says to Mr. Bailey, "You've been given a great gift, George: A chance to see what the world would be like without you." George is in disbelief. He searches inside his trouser pockets for the flower petals his daughter, Zuzu, gave him earlier in the night, proof that he wasn't dreaming. Zuzu's petals are not there because George never existed.

Just think of it: after you've lived a reasonable portion of your life, having the opportunity to look back at your community and the lives of those people in it as if you never existed. Could we recognize our own footprint on this planet? What a blessing it would be to look at our world and see if we made a positive difference in the lives of our brothers and sisters around the world . . . now that's a gift.

George gets to see what his hometown of Bedford Falls would have been like without generous George. There would be no more Bedford Falls—it would have been taken over by Potter and renamed Pottersville. The loving and caring town would have been filled with sin and debauchery. George never would have saved his little brother Harry's life when they were kids, and then his brother Harry never would have saved the lives of other soldiers in the war through his heroism. George wouldn't have been there to keep Mr. Gower from filling out a fatally wrong prescription for a customer. George wouldn't have been able to help people keep their homes and businesses in times of hardship. George wouldn't have been able to help any of his fellow townspeople.

If George had never been born, not only the community of Bedford Falls, but the lives of so many people around the world would have been terribly altered. George's footprint was recognizable.

His guardian angel, Clarence, appeals to George's soul, "Strange, isn't it? Each man's life touches so many other lives. When he isn't around he leaves an awful hole, doesn't he?"

Without George Bailey, life would have been different for so many people. Without George Bailey, evil would have taken over and choked out the true spirit of a loving community. Without George Bailey, life in Bedford Falls would have been far from wonderful.

I wish I were like George Bailey.

I wish for a life where I know I always have a positive effect on others, a life that is always good, a life without temptation or sin, a life without tears of sadness or pain, a life where I only impact others for better and never for worse. A life where I don't have to worry about my children when they leave the house, a life where I am the best husband, father, son, brother, and neighbor I could be, a life full of big smiles, a life where truth is reality and reality is truth, a life where mistakes are forgiven and the Golden Rule is The Rule, a life where a handshake is stronger than a written contract. A life where I can look back and have no regrets, a life where I know that I have made this world a better place to live, a life where I can recognize my footprint.

Sometimes I feel like George Bailey, but only sometimes, and not nearly enough.

At the end of the movie, on Christmas Eve, George is transformed into a new man with the visionary gift of *what if* through Clarence's persistent care. George eventually finds his way back to the Bailey house where his four loving children are waiting. However, his loyal wife, Mary, is not there.

She soon enters after telling everyone in Bedford Falls, all of whom George has helped at one time or another, what has happened to his failing business and the potential trouble ahead. The people he positively impacted come to his rescue with money and love, saving the business and keeping George out of jail. It is the very thing I hope my neighbors would do for me if I were in his shoes.

At the end of the movie, his family and friends, singing "Auld Lang Syne," surround George. His brother, Harry, lifts his glass to toast George and says, "A toast to . . . the richest man in town." As the film closes, he is presented with a gift someone left for him. It's a present from Clarence, a copy of *The Adventures of Tom Sawyer* by Mark Twain, reminding him just how wonderful his life truly is. The handwritten inscription says,

Dear George:—
Remember <u>no</u> man is a failure who has <u>friends</u>. Thanks for the wings!
Love, Clarence

I want to be like George Bailey.

::::::

At a church youth gathering at my house, a high school senior, Chris McCauley, pulled me aside and asked when I had some spare time if I would read his essay he would be submitting with his college applications. His essay was about inspiration and the person that has inspired him the most in his eighteen years. I previously had the privilege of leading him on two mission trips to New Orleans that I initiated and organized. I was flattered that he wanted *me* to read it. Chris's letter read:

> According to Wikipedia there are 17 definitions that refer to the word "inspiration." Like the many definitions Wikipedia has, I can think of many times that have and continue to inspire me. Typing this makes me think of the people, times, and places I have seen and been inspired by. All of it comes to me through an elaborate web of memories that show places, moments, stories, and actions. Having thought about inspiring times in my life, I realized that there's a similar pattern in each inspiration. The time, the environment, the person, the story, and the effect. In most cases, people telling stories or teaching usually forms a strong bond of learning that I grasp. Here is my greatest

moment of inspiration using the pattern I described. The time was Thanksgiving of last year when a couple families from our church used a holiday break to go help with the rebuilding in New Orleans from hurricane Katrina. The best part was getting to share our Thanksgiving meal with Reverend Charles Duplessis and his family and friends in the Lower Ninth Ward. That morning we woke up, and headed down to the Reverend's home. As we were driving through the Lower Ninth Ward and looking at the untouched destruction left over from the storm four years earlier, I thought "how can they ever recover?" The environment was far from inspiring; instead it was very depressing and sad.

We soon arrived at the Reverend's beautifully rebuilt home. During our time together we listened to the Reverend along with his family and friend's personal stories of the storm. They all had lost almost everything they owned and loved. Reverend Duplessis lost his church, his house, personal items, and even people close to him. Through all of the loss and destruction, each one of them remained happy and never lost faith. As we left his home we drove back through the Lower Ninth Ward. As I looked out the window I noticed this once depressing and sad environment drastically changed into the most inspiring landscape I had ever seen. I realized that the people's hope and caring for one another was the key to the rebuilding of their once flooded city. Through this I have been inspired in many different ways. Whether it's talking to a friend that needs hope and love or picking myself up after a bad math test. My life has been altered because of stories I heard in an environment I once thought was hopeless.

I believe that inspiration itself is a gift of hope and power. It is a form of energy spread by someone or something that affects a person in a productive and positive way. Having received this from people who received inspiration of their own, I wish to spread this positive energy to everyone around me. This is my inspiration; this is what I want to give.
(Chris McCauley, 2010)

My heart glowed. My heart also laughed. When Chris first told me he wanted me to read his essay on inspiration, my ego was convinced it was about me. After I read it, I was proud of Chris but ashamed of my ego; my name wasn't visibly written on the paper.

The essay forced me to see Chris through the eyes of George Bailey. If I had never lived, then Chris would not have had the experience in New Orleans that changed his life and inspired him to take action to care for the greater good of his brothers and sisters.

I couldn't see my name, but I could see my footprint.

It's not about me—it's about what I do with me.

Sometimes I feel like George Bailey. . . .

Epilogue: When Hurricanes Shout

We weren't taking the storm seriously until Saturday evening.
—Reverend Charles Duplessis[52]

THE BATTLE FOR MY SOUL raged for 42 years and 18 days; a lifetime of spiritual questioning, degrading labels, battles of good versus evil, and a searching heart circled by my swirling soul like a destructive force of nature. The winds of the tempest would cast me in a wayward direction while the storm surge would bring me right back to where I was, enlightened but still frustrated because I couldn't process the truth of the moment. I wasn't making any ground.

Sometimes my heart was nurtured and grew toward the sun like a beautiful spring flower, blossoming after a gentle rain. Other times the once life-giving and cleansing rain would rush so swiftly that it choked the breath from my lungs and pushed me toward drowning. Too much of any good thing, if delivered in the wrong manner, can be deadly.

I wanted truth! Clear truth! God's Truth! When would the storm end? When could I see the truth and have the serenity that I saw in others? When? Why? Where? Why not? Who? How? I wanted the peace in my heart that I knew "he has" or "she has" or "they have." Why was the storm tormenting me? I was battered and bruised from the push and pull of the rip current that left me with a lack of understanding, a lack of breath. Good on one side of me and evil on the other, both with a lethal hold of my heart and both fighting for the key to my soul. The storm raged. When would I have the answer? When would it be over?

And then there was calm.

I opened my eyes and I watched. I cleared my ears and I listened. The Truth! I saw it. I heard it. Truth rested within my heart. I was saved from the storm.

Calm.

But just as I thought the storm was over, I could see a wall of clouds on the horizon. I looked up to the sky and I could see directly through to the center of heaven right into the heart of God. But then the storm roared back and the winds picked up and the rain pelted my soul with a vengeance even more severe and dangerous than before.

When I thought I was safe and had the answer to my eternal question, I soon realized I was in the eye of the hurricane. A place where safety is only an illusion, a place where I thought I could rest. I didn't want to fight anymore. I just wanted peace.

I couldn't stay in the eye of the storm forever because I knew it would eventually collapse on top of me and destroy everything I fought to gain. The only way to completely get out of the eye of the hurricane is to push through the wall to the other side: a force stronger, swifter, and potentially more deadly than the first part of the tempest.

Flooding rain, tidal surge, and devastating winds hurled ordinary objects through the air at the speed of light. Ordinary objects were lethal bullets if I stood directly in their path.

I became overwhelmed and I knew I couldn't fight any longer. I felt myself getting weaker with every tug on my soul. I knew I was going to die.

It's beyond the deepest terror when you first think you are going to die.

As you see the tree branch breaking, the same one that filtered life-giving oxygen, and realize it is going to land on your body, and when your lungs begin to fill with life-giving water only to grasp that it is now going to choke out your last breath, that is precisely the moment to move swiftly and hold your breath.

I fought the storm, I saw calm in its eye, and I battled through the backside. I knew if I could make it back from a sure death, God could use me to ignite a spark in the darkness where lost souls reside. He could use me to toss out a life preserver when others appear to be drowning. Some people will blow out the spark while others will refuel the flame. Some people sink away from the life preserver while others will fight and grab a hold with their left hand and rescue other souls with their right.

Even though the storm had dissipated and a new life was on the horizon, there was a path of destruction that followed the hurricane, a swath so wide and scarring that it appeared it would take a lifetime to heal. Possessions were destroyed, friends were lost, and painful memories were served at every meal. But there was an odd peace.

Calm.

Truth.

Just because the storm was over didn't mean there wasn't a lot of cleanup to do.

Just because the storm was over didn't mean we would all sit around the campfire Indian-style and sing "Kum Ba Yah."

Just because the storm was over didn't mean the fight was over. There would still be storms, there would still be battles, and there would still be recovery. It's important to always take the storm seriously.

The one thing I did know for certain was that no matter how bad the hurricane, I can make it through to the other side. In the storm, I had found the Truth that I was looking for so desperately.

In the storm, I was healed.

Acknowledgments

THE OLD SAYING THAT GOD works in mysterious ways is a mammoth understatement. As I first sat down and began to write my journey of faith, I had no idea where the words would take me. I had an idea, but I didn't fully realize the impact that so many people have had on my life. It became clear that the closest people to me had an undeniable faith that helped mold the person I am today; they all helped fill my faith balloon. Some of them are friends, foes, family, business associates, or simply people I have casually interacted with. Others I truly believe are angels and saints that God strategically positioned in my life. All of them are important and no different than the ones God arranges in your life. Of course there are countless other people not described in this book or listed here in the acknowledgements that played pivotal roles in my life that helped shape who I am; for all of you I am thankful.

So, to God, I owe You my life. Thank You.

My mother and father, Adeline and Robert Krcelic. They have been the model of resilience. Through good times and bad, they have always been there to love and guide me through whatever difficulties life thrust into my path. They always believed in me, no matter what bone-headed decision I would make. Too many times I rejected their advice, full of wisdom and experience, to follow my own half-witted judgment. Almost every time their advice would have been better accepted and used, rather than rejected. But they let me meander on my own way and welcomed me back without ever saying "I told you so." (It sounds biblical to me!) I now realize that every person must make their own mistakes to truly benefit from life's lessons. Mom and Dad, thank you for the gift of life and for being the parents that you are. I will always love you.

Caroline and Alexis. My two daughters are children that parents dream of having the privilege of raising. Not that they haven't tested me from time to time and still do, as all parents know, but raising my two girls has given me hope for the generations after me. They have shown a love for Christ at such an early age that it has served as an example to me along my own faith journey. They seem to "get it." They understand that every life is fragile, and they have an uncanny social consciousness to help their six billion siblings scattered across the globe. They have helped me realize the love that God the Father had and has for His Son, Jesus of Nazareth. My love for them is unconditional and boundless. Caroline and Alexis, thank you for being who you are. My love for you will never cease.

My siblings, Bobby, Louie, and Tammy. As the baby of the family, I was able to learn from my older brothers and sister at every turn. They never led me astray, while I was able to learn from their mistakes and their accomplishments. I don't even mind that my brother Louie let me get the spanking when it was his idea to roll the Volkswagen Bug down the driveway, ultimately smashing into Mom and Dad's Buick parked on the street (I just had to get that one in). We are all very different with varying views on life and faith. But we all share a love for each other that never waivers. Bobby, Louie, and Tammy, thank you for holding my hand. I have the deepest respect and love for each of you.

A deep thanks to Steve Seman and my other brothers in Christ who took that first mission trip to Bayou LaBatre, Alabama: Marvin

Quattleman Jr., Hugh McVeety, David O'Dell, Jimmy Wright, Bob Coleman, Bob Albright, and Ed Loftis; and to everyone who has since shared their lives and mission experience with me.

Thanks to Gary Gentry and Roy Morgan for giving me a chance of a lifetime with Premier. Shane Quick, John Sanders, and the rest of Christ's warriors at Premier are amazing. Thanks to everyman's role models: Steve Biondo and Ben Mathes, who are the epitome of Paul meets Indiana Jones.

My spiritual mentors, Dan Collins, Tim Roberson, and David Martin gave of themselves in so many ways to help sustain my life and my spirit; I can never thank them enough for being a guiding light during my walk. Reverend Charles Duplessis, who exemplifies the rock of faith, thank you. Thanks to Deb Richardson, who gave me a shot from the pulpit and who truly does God's work every day. Cheryl Staton, who was my guardian angel, protecting me and loving me at all times. My business partner David Wyatt, who jumped in feet-first and walked with me side by side through spiritual battles that taught me invaluable lessons. My appreciation is strong for Noel Golden, Edwin McCain, Jon Murray, Marcus Suarez, Russell Rockwell, Will Merritt, Howard Hudson, and everyone who interned, worked, and invested in OMG. Recognition and appreciation to Paul Marshall, Horace and Walter Turnbull, Jack Frasher, Toby Nelson, Danny Aul, Ben Matthews, Kevin Scott, Thomas Dickerson, and Steve Williams. Much gratitude is given to our clients who believed in us as much as we believed in them.

Thanks to Heidi Wright, who worked closely with me and led my family to Fourth Presbyterian Church; Derrick Quattlebaum, who asked (told) me to be a deacon against my will; my most appreciated high school teacher Mrs. Ruth Boswell for giving me the appreciation for literature and writing; Peter Sullivan, who tried early on to show me the love Christ holds for me; Rob Rogers and Rhonda Pulliam, who served as beacons of light when I didn't believe; Rodney Durham, who continues to walk a Paul-like faith; Gwen Lauderdale, who has endured more than most of us could ever imagine; George Rogers, who has been a good friend and who has set a solid example of bouncing back from adversity; Raymond Newsom for teaching me the art to sales; EMI CMG for believing in us; Jim Zumwalt, Jeff McClusky, Cliff Bartow, and Bob Buford. Rick Turner and John Robinson with PDA for their trust in me to become a part of the National Response Team; Chasen Callahan and the band Chasen; Al and Laura Nardone, who force-fed me with a band I didn't want to listen to but was a pivotal point in opening my eyes and ears to Christian music; Andy Arnold, who coined the term "Satan's Radar"; Geoff Wasserman for the encouragement to stop procrastinating and finish writing; Scott Price for setting the standard for writing excellence; and Jerry Falwell for impacting my wonder years.

Thanks to the Christian music community in Nashville for welcoming a fledgling Christian music executive and record label; Marty Wheeler, who taught me and stood as an example of rebirth; Peter York, Chris Hauser, Joey Elwood, tobyMac, Mac Powell, and the rest of the Christian artists that shout daily praises for God in their music and lyrics.

Gracious thanks to my entire family at Fourth: my pastors Allen McSween, Buz Wilcoxon, David Lindsay, Wain Wesbury, Todd Speed, Trish Gwinn, and all of the other ministers who have touched my life, the Gofourthers and the truly wise members at Fourth Church, all of the young ladies I coached in basketball, and my congregation of brothers and sisters. For the memory of Jack Huffman and to the honor of Molly Beth and Harold. And thanks to everyone who has taken part in my faith journey. I am eternally grateful.

Thanks to my close group of Christian brothers: Don Jackson, Mark Ratchford, Jamey King, Andy Coburn, Tyler Amey, Scott Jones, Scott Ross, Kenworth Reeves, Ken Reeves, and every one of my brothers who will give the shirt off their back with a simple request. And to everyone whose name I may have inadvertently left out . . . thank you!

A special thank you to Tim Lowry and everyone at Ambassador International for believing in this project.

With loving appreciation to John and Nancy Fields for giving birth to and nurturing my wife as a child. I hope I lived up to your expectations.

And finally, I thank my wife, Mary. Her faith has been a guiding light for more than half of my life. Her consistent encouragement has given me the strength to climb the highest hills while helping me through the lowest valleys. Her dedication as a loving mother and loving wife is unparalleled. I can't thank God enough for intersecting our lives on the UNC Chapel Hill campus. Mary, sorry for coming to bed at 3:00 a.m. on numerous occasions and waking you up after hours of writing. I am eternally grateful for your loving support and for encouraging me to finish writing this book. I couldn't have written it without you. I will forever love you!

Endnotes

1   Trevor Hall, "House," Trevor Hall Music, 2009.

2   www.brainyquote.com (accessed 2010).

3   Dickinson, "Because I Could Not Stop for Death," 1863, lines 1–2.

4   www.thinkexist.com (accessed 2010).

5   www.quotationsbook.com (accessed 2010).

6   Tennyson, "Ulysses," 1833, line 18.

7   Freddy Mercury, "We Are the Champions," 1977, Universal Music.

8   www.brainyquotes.com (accessed 2010).

9   2010.

10   Bob Jones, www.jbhe.com, 2009 (accessed 2010).

11   Ibid.

12   www.thethoughtfulchristian.com (accessed 2008).

13   John 13:34–35 (NIV).

14   www.great-quotes.com (accessed 2010).

15   Fourth Presbyterian church bulletin, Greenville, SC, September 5, 2010.

16   Mac Powell, "Cry Out to Jesus," Provident Label Group, 2005.

17   All posts: www.caringbridge.org.

18   Ira Chernus, "Did Bush Say God Told Him To Go To War?" June 30, 2003, http://www.commondreams.org/views03/0630-04.htm (accessed 2010).

19   Exodus 12:1–11 (NIV).

20   2 Corinthians 12:8 (NIV).

21   www.thinkexist.com (accessed 2010).

22   Aaron Shust, "Give Me Words To Speak," Brash Music, 2007.

23   http://blueandgraytrail.com/event/Gettysburg_Address_%5BFull_Text%5D (accessed March 28, 2011).

24   http://www.americanrhetoric.com/speeches/mlkihaveadream.htm (accessed March 28, 2011).

25   "Walt Disney Famous Quotes," The Walt Disney Company, 1994 (accessed 2010).

26   Thomas Dickerson, "Calling All the Nations," OMG Records, 2007.

27   www.thinkexist.com (accessed 2010).

28   Richard Earl Simmons III, *The True Measure of a Man* (The Center for Executive Leadership, 2009).

29   Deuteronomy 34:1–5 (NIV).

30   Jill Devine, "Timing Is Everything," November 27, 2003, http://www.authorsden.com/visit/viewArticle.asp?id=12340 (accessed March 28, 2011).

31   Bob Buford, *Halftime: Moving from Success to Significance* (Grand Rapids: Zondervan, 2008).

32   Bruce L. Shelley, *Church History in Plain Language* (Nashville: Thomas Nelson, 2008).

33   Hope Disaster Relief Mission Statement, 2009.

34   See note 31.

35   See note 31.

36   Ben Harper, "With My Own Two Hands," EMI Virgin Records America Inc., 2003.

37   www.thethoughtfulchristian.com, 2008 (accessed 2010).

38   D'Ann R. Penner and Keith C. Ferdinand, "Overcoming Katrina," 2009 (accessed 2010).

39   www.thethoughtfulchristian.com, 2008 (accessed 2010).

40   Richard Stearns, *The Hole in Our Gospel* (Nashville: Thomas Nelson, 2009).

41   "Like Father Like Son," anti-smoking PSA, 1967.

42   Matthew 7:17–20 (NIV).

43   John 15:1–17 (NIV).

44   Jeanne Brooks, "Alexis Wants to 'Cook It Forward,'" *The Greenville News*, March 20, 2010.

45   www.brainyquote.com (accessed 2010).

46   Brandon Heath, "Give Me Your Eyes," Provident Label Group LLC, 2008.

47   www.theamericaninterview.com, Interview with David Frost, November 1995.

48   www.theamericaninterview.com, *Time* Magazine, January 13, 1996.

49   Toby Mac, "One World," ForeFront Records, 2007.

50   Bill Draper, "James Naismith's Original Basketball Rules Go to Auction in December," Oct. 28, 2010, www.breitbart.com (accessed 2010).

51   *It's a Wonderful Life*, Republic Entertainment Inc., 1946.

52   See note 38.

THE PREMIER FOUNDATION IS A 501 (c)(3) public foundation committed to fulfilling the mission of spreading the gospel of Jesus Christ. With the cooperation of the Premier Group
(Premier Productions, Premier Christian Cruises, Premier Festivals,
and Camp Electric), the Premier Foundation touches millions of
people every year through Christian concerts, cruises, radio, and
other Christ-centered events.

Founding Premier Group owners Roy Morgan and Gary Gentry created the non-profit ministry to support various missionary
activities. Gary and Roy believed it was important to fund activities that feed, clothe, and shelter the poor as well as grant funds to
other charitable activities. The Foundation has grown to expand
its reach by providing grants to some of the world's most diligent
Christian ministries. By growing the Foundation through generous
gifts and creative partnerships, they are able to bless other organizations that are on the front line of healing and hope. They seek to
multiply the resources gifted to them so that God's love reaches
every corner of the globe. Some of those organizations benefit-
ing from the Premier Foundation have included The James Fund,
World Vision, Compassion International, Gospel Music Association
Foundation, Back2Back, Motor Racing Outreach, Rivers of the

World, KLOVE Foundation, World Hope, Holt International, Youth Music Outreach, FamilyLife, Porter's Call, Skip1, Hands and Feet Project in Haiti, and Ciudad de Angeles in Cozumel.

The Premier Foundation's call is found in John 15:12: "My command is this: Love each other as I have loved you." They do this by offering grants to organizations that also love God's children. The Foundation is eternally focused to reach and enrich the work of organizations that embody the gospel of Jesus Christ.

To make a donation or learn more about the Premier Foundation and the Premier Group of companies, go to *www.premierfoundation.com*. Also learn more about Premier's annual fundraising gala, The Champions of the Faith Awards and Benefit Concert, at *www.thechampionsofthefaith.com*.

James Fund. 1:27

a Family Christian Stores Foundation

THE JAMES FUND IS A not-for-profit ministry of Family
Christian Stores. Our mission is found in James 1:27, which says
"pure religion is this: to look after orphans and widows in their
distress." Our passion is to serve our Lord and Savior Jesus Christ
by transforming the lives of orphans and widows in the United
States and in other parts of the world. In His Word, God calls on
His Church—you and me—regarding the orphan and widow to
maintain their cause, to defend them, to execute justice for them, to
not forget them, to lift them up, to deliver them, to come to them,
to hear them, and to be their helper. These are specific promises
God makes to the orphan and widow, and these promises drive
The James Fund forward.

We provide:
- hands-on care through mission trips in the U.S. and Latin America
- adoption assistance grants to key ministry partners
- financial resources to assist in quality of life improvements
- and help for equipping both churches and individuals with
  tools and resources needed to start orphan care and widow
  care ministries of their own.

God has shown His grace and favor to The James Fund, increasing our reach over the past eight years by allowing us to serve in more countries and touch more lives than ever before. And while we see progress, greater things are still to be done.

Lord willing, God's church will rise to greater levels of commitment and individuals like you will join us in partnership to pursue the orphan and widow—knowing that God's glory is revealed through us as we serve.

God is at work. His is bringing hope and joy, giving peace, and restoring lives. Greater things are yet to come and greater things are still to be done on behalf of the orphan and widow.

Join Us. Learn more at *JamesFund.org*.

ABOUT THE AUTHOR

GENE KRCELIC IS THE PRESIDENT of the Premier Foundation, a global Christian charity committed to fulfilling the mission of spreading the gospel of Jesus Christ and dedicated to granting money to worthwhile Christian ministries around the world. Before joining Premier, Gene served as Founder and CEO of OMG SportsEntertainmentMusic, a multi-faceted music, sports, sponsorship, and event management firm with offices in South Carolina, North Carolina, and California. Gene has volunteered his time and resources extensively in disaster relief as well as global Christian ministry. He earned dual degrees from The University of North Carolina at Chapel Hill. Gene lives with his wife, Mary, in Powdersville, South Carolina, and is blessed with two beautiful daughters.

For more information about
Gene Krcelic
&
Loves Like a Hurricane
please visit:

www.loveslikeahurricane.com
@Krcelic
www.facebook.com/genekrcelic

For more information about
AMBASSADOR INTERNATIONAL
please visit:

www.ambassador-international.com
@AmbassadorIntl
www.facebook.com/AmbassadorIntl